What Happened to Obeying the GOSPEL?

Recovering a Treasure From God's Word

Bradley A. Riley

What Happened to Obeying the GOSPEL?

Recovering a Treasure From God's Word

Bradley A. Riley

BAR Publishing

Copyright © 2010 by Bradley A. Riley

First published in the United States of America in 2010 by BAR Publishing

Riley, Bradley A.
What Happened To Obeying The Gospel?
Restoring a Treasure From God's Word

ISBN 978-0-615-35453-8

Printed in the United States of America

*To all who hunger
for more of God…*

Never stop.

*Blessed are those who hunger and thirst for
righteousness, for they shall be satisfied.
(Matthew 5:6)*

CONTENTS

PREFACE

Dear Friend,

For as long as I can remember, I've been a believer in Jesus Christ. I was taught about Him by my mother and grandmother from the time I was small. I understood Jesus was God's Son that died on the cross for my sins, was buried in a borrowed tomb and rose from the dead on the third day. Even though I confessed it, believed it, and faithfully attended church, the life-changing experience I desperately needed never happened. When I was fifteen, I'd had enough; church had become empty and disappointing—so I left.

During the next eight years, a lot of anger, rebellion, sin, and worldliness that was pent up inside began to erupt. Underneath though, I always knew I needed something the world couldn't provide. I wanted to experience God, but I didn't know how. All I knew was to believe in Jesus and the gospel message, and attend church. When I did this I felt as if I could somehow say, "I did my duty." However, that hadn't worked so well, as it never filled the painful void in my heart.

Through college things went on as before, but after graduation, everything changed. When I got my first job, I struck up a good rapport with a Christian coworker named Calvin. After time had passed, he asked if he could interest me in a Bible study. I had always enjoyed reading and learning, so I agreed. I'll never forget how I felt as I listened to those first lessons. I would soon find out what had been missing from all my years of church going. What I saw and experienced wonderfully changed my life.

What I discovered was very "good news" indeed. If you find yourself thinking, as I did, "I wonder if there's more to God than what I've received and learned so far," it's quite likely that God has planted this curiosity in your heart to nudge you along in your pursuit of Him. My hope is that God will use this book to reveal something from His Word that has always been on its pages, but you may not have seen or experienced before.

If you discover previously unnoticed biblical truth as you read this book, don't hesitate to go for it. Since there's always more from God to receive, maybe the Lord has brought you to this point in your relationship to reveal another step in your journey together.

If you're thinking, "What could this guy know that I haven't heard before? I've got the same Bible he has." True—but have you ever been reading a passage in the Bible you've already read many times when something you've never noticed before suddenly springs off the page into your heart? When this happens it's as if the Lord is doing what He did for the disciples in Luke 24:45: opening their understanding to what the Word declared all along—but they didn't recognize until it was their time. It wasn't that they doubted what He'd been telling them, they were merely in a normal process of development, and the Lord knew it was time for them to receive more. I believe God wants to give all of us these special moments in our walk with Him. Why not ask Him for this kind of experience as we explore the wonderful subject of obeying the gospel?

Thanks for investing time to explore what the Bible has to say about this important topic and what it means for us today. My prayer is that we will all continue growing together in Christ and His Word until our departure or His arrival.

Your servant,

Bradley A. Riley

INTRODUCTION

It's the greatest love story of history: "God so loved the world that He gave His only begotten Son, that whosoever believes in Him should not perish, but have eternal life." God personally came in the likeness of human flesh, lived and grew as one of us, gave Himself to the cruel death of crucifixion, was buried, and rose again to life just three days later. It wasn't just to prove He could do it, but to take the penalty for our sinfulness and provide us with the hope of an everlasting life with Him. What we find in His dying, burial and rising again is an unmistakable pattern for us to believe in and follow today.

The gospel message is Jesus' death, burial, and resurrection, and this is very good news! If we're going to proclaim any message to a lost world, this is the one. There's none other with the power to save us from our sins. We can't rely on church-attendance or religion to make us ready for heaven, but putting our hope in the gospel of Jesus Christ will.

This book investigates a very well established biblical practice, but one that is not often closely considered today. To aid in our exploration of obeying the gospel, I'd like to challenge you to put yourself in the shoes of the first post-resurrection believers who placed their faith in the gospel of Jesus Christ. Consider their examples of applying His life-giving message, and always love and esteem God's Word above what anything else has to say.

It is true that we live in perilous times. Second Timothy 3 even informs us that in the last days people will ever be learning, but sadly unable to arrive at the knowledge of the truth. As the return of Christ approaches, it's more important than ever for believers to consistently deepen their level of discipleship to avoid falling into this trap. The good news is that if you're investing the time to read about this subject, you probably already have one of the most important ingredients to prevent this learning dilemma; a very real and God-given hunger for more of His Word. Don't ever let the enemy steal this priceless trait from your life.

Filters

Filters are designed to keep contaminants out of things like water, living environments, cars and furnaces. If these areas need such important protection, how much more do we also need spiritual filters to keep Satan's influence out of our hearts and minds? Because of this, it's always best to filter thoughts, influences and concepts through God's Word, ensuring protection from what our enemy wants to throw in. There is definitely no better filter for life and spiritual battle than the Bible.

This is important because it can be very tempting to rely on someone else's relationship with God to serve as our primary spiritual filter, rather than our own relationship with Him and knowledge of His Word. It can be so easy to count on church attendance or just "believing" to filter our lives. My own experience underlines the fact that these filters won't always get the job done. I had a believing mother and grandmother to help me, but their relationship with God didn't work so well on keeping sin out of my life. They taught me to believe in God, but that didn't keep me from being drawn in the wrong direction. Maybe your experience has taught you the same thing; there's no substitute for a personal connection with Jesus Christ and His Word.

On the other hand, consider the possibility that our spiritual filters can potentially keep things out that God wants to put in. This happened in the Bible with the Pharisees. These religious experts were so convinced of their own righteousness and understanding of Scripture that Jesus Christ Himself couldn't get through to them. (See Matthew 23) Talk about a powerful filter!

The truth is that God always desires to get more and more of His will and Word into our lives, while Satan constantly fights to keep these things out. Let us ask God to give us the wisdom to be aware of our personal filters and to adjust them when necessary to make sure they keep wrong things out and let right things in. If this sounds reasonable, a simple prayer to invite this might go something like; "Jesus, I confess I don't know everything there is to know about You, and I want to know more. Please keep my eyes open to continue discovering wonderful things in your Word, and always help me to respond with faith and obedience. Help me not to allow Satan to keep good things from me, because I want to receive everything You want me to have. I ask these things in Jesus' name. Amen."

Sincerity

Before going any further, we need to take a moment to address an item of great importance. While *What Happened to Obeying the Gospel* is designed to be a challenging and informative exploration of the subject at hand, it is not intended to bring anyone's Christian sincerity into question. There is little doubt of the genuineness in anyone's relationship with God who invests time to study His Word and faithfully draw closer to Him. This book merely attempts to love and present more of the good news it is possible to have—and more of His good news is definitely a good thing.

Without doubt, sincerity is indispensable to true Christianity—but sincerity has another side. It's possible to hold sincerely to beliefs and traditions even when they are different from biblical precedent. If, while reading God's Word, we discover a discrepancy between what we're reading and what we're actually believing and doing, it doesn't mean we're insincere. Neither does it cancel out our faith and relationship with God. On the contrary, it probably means we cared enough to search the Scriptures for proof of our beliefs—and that a loving God also cares enough to share more of Himself with us. Our simple willingness to act upon what His Word shows then becomes the real test of our sincerity.

Unashamedly, this book boldly stands up for the foundational biblical practice of obeying the gospel. It isn't meant to be offensive to any believer, and I pray it does not come across that way to you. If it seems that concepts are presented strongly, the intention is merely to "contend earnestly for the faith which was once for all handed down to the saints." (Jude 1:3)

In a world that is becoming increasingly less tolerant of anything the Bible has to say, I hope this kind of stand is welcome and refreshing.

1

THE FOUNDATION OF OBEYING THE GOSPEL

Accepting Jesus Christ

Of all the Bible topics to study, receiving Jesus Christ as Lord and Savior is the most eternally significant, and certainly deserves our careful attention. We know that the gospel is the good news of Jesus' death, burial, and resurrection, but how does one receive this gift of salvation through His act of love and power? The biblical record clearly shows people being saved as they responded to the good news. This book will carefully examine their pattern of faith. You might be quite surprised to see that these clear and repeated examples are very different from methods commonly taught and practiced today.

Even though many sincere believers may not be aware of, or currently follow the biblical blueprint of obeying the gospel, all over the world we can find present-day examples of leaders discovering and joyfully applying this scriptural pattern. One such individual is Bishop John C. Wayabire, senior pastor of Revival and Salvation Church of God Ministries, who shepherds a flock of over one million believers in Uganda and surrounding East African nations. I met this humble servant of God in the summer of 2008 and was privileged to hear him recount his wonderful story of discovery.

As of December 2008, Bishop Wayabire's leadership covered over one thousand churches, nearly two thousand ministers, approximately eighty-five hundred orphans, and more than four thousand widows. While these figures are extraordinary, he told me how he discovered that something was missing from his ministerial practice. One day this highly successful spiritual leader discovered that he had not fully obeyed the gospel.

He came to this meaningful understanding in December 2006, during a trip to the United States. At first, he wrestled with what he saw in the Scriptures, but finally decided to demonstrate simple faith by obeying what God showed him he had yet to do. Perhaps you might recognize the same opportunity to receive and apply more of the good news. If so, it might be a struggle initially, but you'll never regret acting upon what God reveals from His Word.

Today, Bishop Wayabire proclaims this exciting biblical discovery to those under his care, and believers are responding by the hundreds of thousands. Not only have people under his own ministry responded, but leaders from other churches who attend his advertised meetings are seeing and receiving more of the gospel as well.

What was it this leader saw that prompted him to respond with new faith to an old and familiar message? The answer to this question underscores the heart and purpose of this book.

As you begin the journey through these pages, I pray you are energized, challenged, informed, and above all, completely obedient to the wonderful good news Jesus came to bring the world. May you know and experience the gospel as never before!

Goals

This undertaking is designed to accomplish several goals that revolve around the scriptural practice of obeying the gospel. In addition to the items outlined below, there are other concepts included to offer additional encouragement in your relationship with God. Here is some of what you'll see:

1. Biblical evidence of the necessity of obeying the gospel of Jesus Christ
2. Examples of the repeated pattern of obeying the good news
3. The contrast between New Testament examples of believers accepting Christ and modern methods of accepting this good news as an act of conversion

4. The need to recover the teaching of gospel obedience through responding to the gospel message as it is consistently demonstrated in the Bible
5. Historical alterations to the original, biblical pattern of gospel application

I'm so grateful for the saving grace provided by the death, burial, and resurrection of Jesus Christ. His sacrifice offers a rescue from sin's grasp that no amount of human works can ever produce. Because of this best of news, we are invited to walk through this saving, open door today. It is truly through Christ alone that we have access to God's merciful salvation.

The importance of not changing the gospel

The gospel is a priceless treasure, something never to be treated casually or neglectfully. God paid such a tremendous price and sacrificed so much to provide it that He clearly doesn't want it altered. Paul wrote about this to Galatian believers who hadn't kept their "filters" maintained and were unwittingly succumbing to wrong influences and ideas. They were in danger of letting the gospel Paul preached to them be polluted by distortions. It's probable that Judaizers had traveled to this Asian province in Paul's wake to persuade the people in this largely Gentile church that even though they had obeyed the gospel of Jesus Christ they now had to obey Jewish law in order to be saved. When Paul heard the news, he wrote to them in distress:

> I am amazed that you are so quickly deserting Him who called you by the grace of Christ, for a different gospel; which is really not another; only there are some who are disturbing you and want to distort the gospel of Christ. But even if we, or an angel from heaven, should preach to you a gospel contrary to what we have preached to you, he is to be accursed! (Galatians 1:3-8)

It would be naïve to think similar scenarios don't happen today. Although some might distort the gospel on purpose, more often than not it's probably because of well-intentioned practices which have been passed down through generations without a thorough and reasonable scriptural examination.

Holding beliefs to the light of God's Word

It is vital for Christians to know exactly what they believe and where in the Bible that belief is established. Though I've listened to many excellent ministers, I don't want to fall into the careless habit of accepting everything I hear without my own biblical examination. Acts 17 gives an example of Berean believers who not only "received the Word with great eagerness," but examined "the Scriptures daily to see whether these things were so." Apparently, they were convinced of the truth that Paul preached because "many of them believed." (See Acts 17:11-12) Careful and prayerful Bible study will always prove or disprove the message we've heard preached.

When it comes to personal beliefs and practices, it's easy to become protective if we perceive they're being questioned. Instead of responding defensively though, a positive reaction can provoke us to dig into the Bible for more truth, and letting Scripture be the authority for any question at hand. Such inquiries can therefore be healthy, with subsequent study allowing us to be "approved to God as a workman who does not need to be ashamed, accurately handling the word of truth." (2Timothy 2:15)

As long as God's Word establishes our belief, it doesn't matter what challenges it. Close examination cannot threaten the integrity of Scripture. This is because inspection never diminishes truth; it only reveals it. Because of this, the opportunity to measure beliefs biblically should be welcomed, so we can understand and subsequently apply more truth to our lives. If such an examination reveals that a belief or practice is short of verifiable biblical precedent, we must have the enthusiasm, courage and faith to obey the Scriptures, even if others don't understand at first. Our faith should fight the complacency that says, "I believe in God," while secretly thinking, "I don't want to have to do anything differently than what I'm already doing."

When God brings something new to our understanding, this is where the enemy would really like us to become offended rather than obedient. Let's never fall into the trap of becoming upset at what we see in our own Bibles and, as some have done, reject the very words they've professed to believe. I would always encourage everyone to ask God to reveal the truths of His Word and then base a response on the biblical evidence He provides.

While reading the Bible passages covered in this book, if you notice verifiable concepts you haven't recognized before, please realize that nothing new has been added. It has been in Scripture all along. When we love and seek truth, God sees our hunger and wants to respond by sharing more of Himself with us. Let us never fail to celebrate and treasure the truths He reveals and be faithful to apply all the discoveries He allows us to receive.

Obeying the gospel—Scripture references

As we explore the Bible references related to obeying the gospel, you will notice that these are not isolated passages, but a theme woven throughout the New Testament. Although some of the references might sound ominous, the intent is merely to bring attention to their presence for the purposes of our study, not to be intimidating. Let's start with a very prominent selection.

The first of three specific references is found in Romans 10, where the apostle Paul expresses frustration because there were those who heard the gospel message but did not obey it. If you have been around Christian culture very long, you've most likely heard verse 13 quoted as what we must do to be saved. What you may not have heard frequent reference to is the charge of obeying the gospel found three verses later. Notice Paul's emphasis of the importance of applying the gospel by obeying the message of Christ's death, burial and resurrection:

> For whosoever shall call upon the name of the Lord shall be saved. How then shall they call on him in whom they have not believed? and how shall they believe in him of whom they have not heard? and how shall they hear without a preacher? And

> how shall they preach, except they be sent? as it is written,
> How beautiful are the feet of them that preach the gospel of
> peace, and bring glad tidings of good things! But they have not
> all obeyed the gospel. For Esaias saith, Lord, who hath
> believed our report? (Romans 10:13-16 KJV)

This begins the heart of our study. What did Paul mean by this statement in verse 16? He equates faith in the gospel message with applying some type of obedience. The audience Paul refers to evidently heard the gospel but did not receive the message by obeying it.

We find the next mention of this phrase in 2Thessalonians. The seriousness of the passage is very sobering, further revealing the importance Scripture places on obeying the gospel:

> To give relief to you who are afflicted and to us as well when
> the Lord Jesus will be revealed from heaven with His mighty
> angels in flaming fire, dealing out retribution to those who do
> not know God and to those who do not obey the gospel of our
> Lord Jesus. These will pay the penalty of eternal destruction,
> away from the presence of the Lord and from the glory of His
> power, when He comes to be glorified in His saints on that day,
> and to be marveled at among all who have believed—for our
> testimony to you was believed. (2Thessalonians 1:7-10)

The apostle Peter also refers to the necessity of obeying the gospel in a third reference:

> For it is time for judgment to begin with the household of God;
> and if it begins with us first, what will be the outcome for those
> who do not obey the gospel of God? (1Peter 4:17)

Clearly, there is a transfer of God's saving righteousness to those obedient to the gospel which is absent for individuals who turn down the opportunity. This isn't a misguided attempt at salvation by believers' works, it is allowing God to impart His salvation and righteousness through the gospel—which is His saving work alone.

While these three passages call attention to the necessity of obeying the good news, it is important to note they do not show anyone actually doing so. We will explore these important biblical examples in detail later. For now, notice the focus of these verses: instead of placing attention on believing the gospel, they address the eternal significance of obeying it. The apostles clearly expected some type of manifestation of faith once someone believed that Jesus Christ died, was buried, and rose again.

Obey the "Faith"

Not only is the phrase "obey the gospel" recorded in Scripture, but many similar passages accompany the term "obey" as it pertains to placing faith in Christ. Acts shows us that "the faith" is also something to obey:

> The word of God kept on spreading; and the number of the disciples continued to increase greatly in Jerusalem, and a great many of the priests were becoming obedient to the faith. (Acts 6:7)

When beginning his letter to the Romans, Paul also mentions this phrase:

> By whom we have received grace and apostleship, for obedience to the faith among all nations, for his name: (Romans 1:5 KJV)

Obviously, these individuals had believed on Jesus Christ, but how did they obey "the faith"? What an opportunity to explore more about the good news!

Obey the "Truth"

Peter states in another related Scripture passage that when we obey "the truth" our souls are purified. You might ask the logical question, "Is obeying the truth the same as obeying the gospel?" We know that Peter believed in obeying the gospel from the previous quote in 1Peter 4, so perhaps he was referring to the same thing. Is there a greater truth than the good news that Jesus

Christ died for our sins, was buried, and rose again on the third day? Judge for yourself:

> Since you have in obedience to the truth purified your souls for a sincere love of the brethren, fervently love one another from the heart, for you have been born again not of seed which is perishable but imperishable, that is, through the living and enduring word of God. (1Peter 1:22-23)

We can be confident that the "truth" Peter spoke about is in fact the gospel message, for Ephesians states the "message of truth" is the gospel of our salvation:

> In Him, you also, after listening to the message of truth, the gospel of your salvation—having also believed, you were sealed in Him with the Holy Spirit of promise. (Ephesians 1:13)

Romans provides yet another mention of obeying the truth:

> To those who by perseverance in doing good seek for glory and honor and immortality, eternal life; but to those who are selfishly ambitious and do not obey the truth, but obey unrighteousness, wrath and indignation. (Romans 2:7-8)

Galatians continues with two additional references:

> O foolish Galatians, who hath bewitched you, that ye should not obey the truth, before whose eyes Jesus Christ hath been evidently set forth, crucified among you? (Galatians 3:1, KJV)

> You were running well; who hindered you from obeying the truth? (Galatians 5:7)

Obey the "Teaching"

Here, yet another reference from Romans relays the message that it was obedience to a certain Christian teaching that set these believers free from sin:

> But thanks be to God that though you were slaves of sin, you became obedient from the heart to that form of teaching to

which you were committed, and having been freed from sin,
you became slaves of righteousness. (Romans 6:17-18)

We can know the gospel was the teaching they obeyed, because
it is what the apostles were charged to proclaim, and what brought
the power of salvation from sin. These readings don't yet show
how the believers obeyed the message—just that they did.

Saved by "Obeying Christ"

In our last reference for this chapter, the writer of Hebrews
recognizes that the Son of God is the source of salvation to those
who will obey Him. In light of the other Scriptures covered so far,
this passage is additional confirmation that believers must obey
His gospel:

> Although He was a Son, He learned obedience from the things
> which He suffered. And having been made perfect, He became
> to all those who obey Him the source of eternal salvation.
> (Hebrews 5:8-9)

Conclusion

We can easily see that throughout the New Testament there is a
consistent theme and requirement of obedience connected to the
good news message. I hope you're curious to see how this truth
plays out in Scripture. As this book unfolds, we will carefully
observe the repeated biblical pattern of obeying the gospel.
Shockingly, it is quite different from the practice of many believers
today. I sincerely pray this work can be an aid to help restore this
practice wherever needed.

As we end this chapter, here is an interesting question to
consider; If Jesus Christ had to personally experience a death, a
burial, and a resurrection before *He* could ascend to Heaven, can
we neglect to identify with any part of His saving example and
expect Heaven to be ours?

2

THE WAR AGAINST RECOVERY

Not a normal thief

The thief comes only to steal and kill and destroy; I came that
they may have life, and have it abundantly. (John 10:10)

While it is true that Jesus is in the business of providing abundant
life and Satan is a thief, it is critical to observe that our enemy is
not just in business to steal, but to also kill and destroy. His
motivation to take his efforts to these lower levels is important to
examine.

What comes to mind when you picture a thief? I think of someone
who seeks valuables to convert into quick cash. I don't think a
normal thief takes something only to destroy it or kill it—but Satan
is the type of thief who does. He desires to take precious truths
away from God's people and eradicate them so they will never be
restored. He wants to steal things which are alive and kill them so
they aren't just missing, but so they are dead to us and eventually
become forgotten. Since he cannot have the things of God, he
doesn't want us to have them either. It's no wonder Jesus called
him a murderer in John 8:44.

God restores until His return

As Satan is actively seeking to steal, kill and destroy, Acts 3 lets
us know that God is in the process of restoring things. This is so
important that heaven must actually keep Jesus until all things are
restored according to Acts 3. Here is the passage:

"Therefore repent and return, so that your sins may be wiped
away, in order that times of refreshing may come from the
presence of the Lord; and that He may send Jesus, the Christ
appointed for you, whom heaven must receive until *the* period

of restoration of all things about which God spoke by the mouth
of His holy prophets from ancient time. (Acts 3:19-21)

What are these "all things" to be restored? While we may not know
all of the answers to this prophetic question, we can always
cooperate with God in this important work by opening our hearts
to everything He desires to re-establish for us personally. Without
a doubt, one of the greatest practices to be restored before
Christ's return is the understanding and practice of obeying the
gospel as demonstrated in the Bible. You may be alarmed to see
how things have changed since the initial pattern of responding to
the good news was established. I remember how deeply surprised
I was after carefully studying the scriptures to discover I had not
completely obeyed the gospel. Perhaps you'll be equally shocked
to come to the same conclusion... and just as excited at the
opportunity to receive and apply more good news.

Robbery victims—angry or indifferent?

Let's get back to the thief. If an intruder took something valuable
from you, how would you react?

Imagine being in this scenario; a thief broke into your house,
shoved you out of the way, grabbed your belongings, and then
yelled as he crawled out the window, "You don't need this stuff
anyway. You'll be just fine without it!" Would you just say, "Okay, if
you say so, mister"? Absolutely not! My guess is you'd probably
do everything you could to prevent the theft and protect your
family from the intruder.

In the following scenarios, robbery victims experience varying
reactions to the crime depending on their perspective. Think about
being in their shoes.

Present

In our first hypothetical example, a thief breaks into your home while you're gone and steals some valuables. When you return, you're very upset to discover your computer, stereo, and firearms are gone. You think, "How dare someone break into my home and take what belongs to me! I hope I get the chance to get it all back! I want to make sure this never happens again!" You feel angry, afraid, violated, and maybe even vengeful. You do everything you can to get your belongings back. Most likely, we all would.

In December of 1994, I experienced such a robbery. I remember the fear and anger I felt when arriving home to a broken-in front door, and discovering items from stereo equipment to Christmas gifts missing. I also remember my strong desire to *recover* what was stolen.

In a spiritual application, what if there was a robbery attempt on the Christian values you hold so dear? Say that a respected spiritual leader in your life publicly stood up one day and made a statement such as, "Jesus really wasn't the Son of God. He was just a good man who established some great guidelines to live by." How would that make you feel? Your feelings might closely parallel the same emotions as the robbery victim above; a strong desire to protect what was threatened, and to restore anyone's faith that had been undermined.

I hope you never experience a thief in your house, naturally or spiritually. If you have, you can probably relate to these feelings. Robberies aren't always this obvious, however, and our reactions can change depending on the circumstances.

Recent past

This time let's look at a robbery from a personal yet more removed perspective. Suppose a treasured print was stolen from your late parents' home fifty years ago. Unexpectedly, you receive a phone call from the authorities: "While we were searching a thief's storage unit, we came across a framed print of a unique painting. We found a small card stuck into the back of the frame that had a name and address. On a chance, we called the current phone number registered to that address. Would you happen to be related to a Henry Anderson? If you know who the former residents of this house were, it would help us locate the owners of the painting so we can return it to the rightful heir."

"Henry Anderson was my father!" you exclaim. "The painting was stolen before I was born! It's been so long ago that I'd forgotten the story about it. But I'd sure like to get it back."

"Can you come to the station to claim it from the evidence room? Bring proof of your ID, preferably a birth certificate and a driver's license."

You would quickly locate these items and jump in your car to head down to the police station, if for no other reason than a healthy curiosity! You would probably be excited and filled with anticipation of a reconnection to your heritage.

What about anger, though? Do you think you would be less angry at the thief who robbed your parents fifty years ago than the one who robbed your house last week? Most likely. It would still be an encounter with a thief, but from a more distant perspective.

What would you feel about the picture once you hung it on your own dining room wall? Even if it wasn't very valuable as far as the art market was concerned, it would almost certainly mean a tremendous amount to you because of the personal connection.

I have an old painting that used to hang in my late grandmother's home. It depicts a secluded pool formed by a small waterfall in a peaceful, wooded setting. In it, a boy and his dog are returning from a fishing trip with a stringer filled with his catch. Just thinking of it brings back many memories. When I was a boy, we had to send my first dog to live on my grandmother's farm because there wasn't enough space at our house. I also spent countless hours fishing in her farm pond through the years. I always looked forward to those weekend and summer visits. While the picture has no great monetary value, I treasure it. I was fortunate to inherit this painting after she passed away in 1996, and it will always have a special place in my heart. Every time I see it, I remember my grandmother and those special times.

Just suppose I wasn't fortunate enough to inherit the picture, but one day I saw a print of it for sale in a gallery. You bet I'd do whatever I could to buy it! The personal connection would obviously affect my eagerness to acquire the item.

On the other hand, what if the painting had been in my family all along but stored away in my grandparents attic throughout my lifetime without my knowledge? It would still be a part of our family's past, but my perception would be quite different. If I saw it at a gallery, I probably wouldn't care much about buying it, even if it was nostalgic or impressive. The absence of a recognized personal connection would naturally affect my attraction to the item.

In a spiritual sense, what if we became aware that a jewel was taken from the treasury of God's Word a generation ago? Would we be curious, grateful, and feel a sense of reconnection with our heritage if given the opportunity to recover it? Would we be angry that someone had taken this from our relatives' relationship with God? More importantly, would we gladly accept the recovered item, and what would we do with it? How would we feel about reclaiming something we may not have known was a part of our family—the body of Christ—after we learned there was undeniable proof? Our perceived personal connection will probably have a lot to do with the level of desire to accept its return.

These are much more eternal and important questions than what we would do with the recovery of mere material possessions. The answers will say a lot about our hearts, and how we treasure God's Word.

Far-removed

What if a precious antique had been stolen from your great-great grandparents and you had the chance to get it back? Maybe it was once prized but now it's been forgotten; you never even knew it existed, much less that your ancestors owned it. What if it had been in your family a dozen generations ago? Would you be eager to claim it, especially if there was proof it rightfully belonged to you? Perhaps, since you didn't experience a personal connection with your great-great grandparents, it might not mean as much as the items in the first two scenarios. You might even be suspicious about the person who found it and doubt that the item really belonged to you. Would you be inconvenienced by the discovery, or would you rejoice over getting the property back?

In this situation, your reaction would probably be less predictable, even if there were proof that the item was rightfully yours. Your desire to have it sitting in your own home would obviously depend on your personal assessment of its value and importance.

What does this mean to us?

The enemy of our souls has always stolen things from mankind. He not only wants to take things that rightfully belong to us, but to do it in such a way that we shrug and think, "We don't need that anyway." He desires to remove old landmarks from God's Word so stealthily that we may not realize they are gone. If someone should discover they are missing, he hopes we react with quick judgments like, "That hasn't been in our family for generations, we don't need it anymore," or "Please don't bother me with this. I'm busy with other things." Not only is the devil attempting to steal our love, knowledge, and deep reverence for the Word of God, he wants to replace it with apathy and indifference, some hallmark characteristics of the last-days generation.

In 2Timothy 4:3, the apostle Paul predicted this kind of thievery in the days before Christ's return; that people wouldn't endure sound teaching. In a fast-paced and convenience-driven culture, the value of enduring anything is sadly becoming a lost art. It's unfortunate that something as indispensable as Bible teaching would fall into this category, especially at this critical time in history. May God help those that trust in Him to keep their hearts open to all the priceless treasures of the Bible, especially since God is in the process of restoring things in preparation for the second coming of Christ.

As God works to bring us more of His Word, we can react to it in various ways. What type of response is He looking for? The answer is in Isaiah 66:2: "To this one I will look, to him who is humble and contrite of spirit, and who trembles at My word."

Do we still tremble at His Word, or has it become familiar or routine? It pleases God when we maintain a reverence for the holiness, purity, and awesomeness of Scripture. If we've lost any of these traits, let's be honest and humble enough to confess this to God and ask that He mercifully restore them.

The thief's reaction

I wonder how happy the thief would be if the rightful heirs of his original robbery victims refused to carefully appraise and reclaim any recovered treasures, or if they dismissively rejected the valuables, even after being presented with legitimate evidence connected to the find. Wouldn't the thief be smug if they became suspicious of the discoverers instead of investigating the legitimacy of their inheritance?

Easy question: What do you think Satan will try to do to us as God attempts to restore things the enemy has stolen from our forefathers? I think the answer will be remarkably close to the John 10 description—to hope he has not only stolen, but also killed and destroyed as well.

What happened, Esau?

An Old Testament episode between twin patriarchal brothers provides an interesting example of how time can rob the desire to recover something taken. As the eldest twin, Esau was the rightful heir to his father Isaac's blessing and birthright. Though they belonged to him, he lost both. OK, technically he traded his birthright for a bowl of beans and was tricked out of his father's blessing by a conspiracy between his mother and his brother, Jacob. Nice family dynamics working there, huh?

It would be easy to blame Esau for being careless and nonchalant about his inheritance and for letting Jacob get the better of him. One might even empathize with his rage toward his trickster brother for stealing his blessing. You can almost feel Esau's anguish as he begged his aged father to somehow return his blessing:

> Then he said, "Is he not rightly named Jacob, for he has supplanted me these two times? He took away my birthright, and behold, now he has taken away my blessing." And he said, "Have you not reserved a blessing for me?" (Genesis 27:36)

When Esau got a watered-down version of the real blessing, he quit crying and his heart hardened. He plotted, "When Father dies, I'm going to kill Jacob!" (See Genesis 27:41)

Jacob heard about his brother's plot and moved far away. As the years passed, Esau's indignation and anger dissipated, though. When Jacob finally returned home, Esau came to meet him, bringing four hundred men. At their reunion, a terrified Jacob offered to return the blessing in the form of an enormous gift, but Esau wasn't interested. Jacob began to relax when Esau acted as if his main interest now was to restore familial fellowship. Esau said, "Keep the gift, brother. I already have enough." (See Genesis 33)

The question that begs to be asked is; what happened to Esau's desire to take back his inheritance? It was gone. Not only had he suffered a profound loss, but now he had also lost the will to recover it.

What does this say about Esau's character? Perhaps it says many things, such as maybe he truly learned forgiveness. It takes less speculation to see that Esau had learned to live without his blessing. With a satisfied heart and mind he told Jacob, "I have plenty, my brother; keep what you have." Esau had forgotten how desperate he once was to recover what rightfully belonged to him.

In our day, learning to live without the promises and blessings God has intended for our generation can have the same effect on us. If we aren't careful, we will lose a healthy desire to reclaim them. A good way to combat this is to keep our spiritual filters in good working order by making room in our hearts for God to restore any truths He wants to. If we feel as if we "already have enough," or can live without it, we may never receive anything more from Him. If we discover something that has been missing, we should carefully appraise it—and by all means, accept God's attempt to give it back.

Hilkiah to Shaphan to Josiah

These three characters in 2Kings 22-23 play the main roles in one of the Bible's best accounts of recovery. This is a tremendous example of a leader discovering truth from the word of God then courageously using his position to reinstate its mandates to those under his care.

King Josiah came to the throne of Judah when he was only eight years old. Along with the throne, he inherited a big mess. His grandfather Manasseh had been terribly wicked, committing all sorts of abominations, including sacrificing one of his sons in the fiery hollow belly of Molech, and setting up a carved image of the goddess Asherah inside the very Temple of God!

After Manasseh, Josiah's father, Amon became king. For two years, things slid further downhill. Inheriting his father's love for the gods of surrounding nations, Amon worshiped at their altars his father had set up inside the Temple. He even permitted houses of male prostitution in or around the Temple. On the high places across the land, people built shrines to the gods and goddesses Chemosh, Milcom and Ashtoreth. Amon's palace servants became so disgusted they assassinated him, and then placed his son Josiah to the throne.

Amazingly, Josiah did what was right in the eyes of the Lord. Somewhere in his life there must've been a Godly influence, though it surely wasn't his father or grandfather. At twenty-six, in the eighteenth year of his reign, he sets out to repair the Temple. He sent his scribe Shaphan to retrieve the building funds from Hilkiah the high priest so workers could begin the renovations. Arriving at the Temple, Shaphan found that Hilkiah had made an interesting discovery inside—he had found the misplaced Book of the Law. He gave it to Shaphan, who in turn brought it to Josiah and read it to him. Unlike his predecessors, Josiah was so moved and convicted by what he heard that he tore his clothes in repentance. Since the reign of Hezekiah, Josiah's great grandfather, the Word had languished, dusty and overlooked in the Temple, even though it had been there all along.

With remarkable courage and zeal, Josiah purged evil and restored God's covenant with Judah. His passion for God and His Word is a masterpiece of recovery from a spiritual robbery—and a blueprint for us to look to today. The highlights of his righteous rampage can be found in 2Kings 22-23.[1]

What a leader!

There are several admirable things in this story. Josiah's righteous actions occurred not because they were convenient, popular, or

---

[1] He has the book read to all the elders of Judah; renews the people's covenant with God; removes all symbols of idolatry from the Temple; tears down the houses of male cult prostitutes; destroys the idolatrous high places and pagan priests; reinstitutes the Passover; and removes the mediums, spiritists, and idols.

easy to do. At first, many people likely resisted the king's reforms, which probably strained some strategic relationships. Things had been comfortable for generations, and now the king was making everything difficult again. This course of action might have even endangered the king's life. His advisors possibly said things like, "You're committing political suicide if you do this, Josiah! You're in a building program and it would be a bad move to start all of this right now."

Josiah was also already eighteen years into his reign when Hilkiah made this Word-discovery. The king could have chosen not to rock the boat and had him send the Book back to the Temple without telling anyone. It was too late, though. The sacred words melted his heart and he couldn't get away from them. Josiah then boldly demonstrated the courage and faith it took to lead his nation into what God had revealed.

Josiah wasn't a people pleaser; he was more interested in being a God pleaser. This type of godly "fear" is rare in modern church culture. Think about it; when was the last time you looked at someone and said, "There goes a person who fears the Lord"? Unfortunately, it is probably becoming increasingly infrequent.

How does the story leave you feeling about Josiah? If I had to sum up my opinion of this king, it would be with one word: respect. Maintaining a life worthy of respect is more valuable than popularity, money or any other thing we could trade for it. What character traits will God look for in a believer or a leader? While there are many, the earlier quote from Isaiah provides one of the most accurate assessments of Josiah—he trembled at God's word.

It might be healthy to ask ourselves; when was the last time we picked up the Bible and discovered something that moved us so much we were determined to implement it, even if it resulted in a temporary loss of the understanding of others?

May God grant us a hunger to reconnect with and apply anything and everything the enemy has stolen, no matter how long ago the robbery was—even if it takes others a while to appreciate it.

The war against recovery

Satan knows how vital obeying the gospel message is, and desperately wants to prevent anyone from doing so. One primary tactic he uses originated in the Garden of Eden. Just as he did to Eve, he tries to deceive us into discounting the validity of God's Word—effectively stealing it. He then knows the longer the time span between the theft and its discovery, the weaker the interest in recovery is likely to be. When someone has no desire to recover something from the Word, it can be difficult for even God to restore it. With the passage of time, Satan wants to thus destroy and kill what he has stolen. May we never let him have this satisfaction in our lives.

Why would believers practice things differently than biblical patterns demonstrate? Perhaps many reasons, but most likely, because it was handed down by a previous generation, which was handed to them by their previous generation, all the way back to when an original practice was changed. Examining traditions doesn't bring one's earnestness into question, it only reveals the foundation of a practice or teaching. If a Christian belief is true, it will stand up to biblical examination without being threatened. Teachings are merely revealed to be true or untrue by this kind of inspection and testing. Our generation is counting on the church to reflect the Word of God consistently and accurately. One way to ensure this happens is by never being afraid of this kind of honest assessment.

When a believer sees there is more of God's Word to have and apply, it isn't an occasion to become defensive (as the enemy would have us react), but rather an opportunity to respond with enthusiasm and faith. It indicates that God has seen one's desire and heart for Him, and that He wants to share more of what He has to offer. As we walk with God, our journey is supposed to be one of continual discovery of more of His love, grace, and truth. God can resurrect and restore things from His Word that were alive to our Christian ancestors. Acts 3:19-21 indicates He will be doing so until Christ's return. We can cooperate with this divine restoration by simply acting on what God reveals. Satan's war against recovery intends to make us too comfortable and set in our traditions to allow this to happen.

Growing (pains) in the grace and knowledge of God

Someone once said, "When we're through growing, we're through." Growth is change, and change is rarely comfortable. Sometimes it is even painful. While being firmly established in the faith is essential, we must never allow past knowledge to prevent us from the additional understanding God desires to give us. It wasn't painless for the disciples to leave their jobs and routines behind to follow the Messiah, but it was absolutely worth it. They grew in ways they couldn't have dreamed of previously. He taught them principles that revolutionized their lives, and then their world.

This didn't mean the twelve were perfect or grasped all of Christ's concepts on the first try. Sometimes it took time for them to catch on. How many times did the Lord tell them He would die and then rise again on the third day, while their understanding couldn't quite grasp it? They finally believed when they saw it for themselves. Many times, it is the same with us. We need to see things for ourselves to believe. When it comes to matters of His Word, we should.

If we notice things firmly established in the Bible that we don't practice today, it can be tough to admit we aren't following what these examples teach, especially if we are a teacher ourselves. The good news is that it can be a God-sent opportunity to lead by example—as Bishop Wayabire continues to do in Africa since he saw there was more of the gospel he could apply.

Hide and seek

Perhaps the greatest journey a believer will ever embark on is the exploration of God's written Word. His Word reveals so many things: His nature, creation, His will for our lives, the past record of human history, and our future destiny. This only scratches the surface of the riches available to us as we explore this eternal treasure we call the Bible. In the same way we must purposefully dig to locate natural treasure, we also must deliberately mine the pages of scripture to discover its available wisdom and instruction.

Why isn't all biblical truth in plain sight, though? The reason is what I like to call God's "hide-and-seek" principle. Proverbs says, "It is the glory of God to conceal a matter, But the glory of kings is to search out a matter." (Proverbs 25:2)

Why would God hide things from us? I think the answer is simply that He's interested in being pursued. If everything about God were painfully obvious, we'd take Him for granted. As humans, we usually have a greater appreciation for things that require time to intentionally investigate, while things merely given to us aren't usually as cherished. Christ's pattern of teaching with parables bears this out. When the meanings weren't obvious, these word pictures gave casual observers an easy opportunity to say, "That doesn't make any sense to me. I'll just move on." Often the parables became clear only when the hearers, usually His closest disciples, stuck around long enough for the opportune time to ask Jesus to explain what the story meant. This is a key to understanding the nature of God. When He observes our determination to understand more, He's happy to share further insights. All we have to do is ask and continue seeking:

> But without faith it is impossible to please him: for he that cometh to God must believe that he is, and that he is a rewarder of them that diligently seek him. (Hebrews 11:6 KJV)

Matthew 13:44 and Luke 15:4-8 provide parables about a man who discovers treasure, a shepherd who finds a lost sheep, and a woman who recovers a lost coin. At the end of each story, the seeker celebrates with great joy. In all three parables, the discoveries were not by accident, but the man, the shepherd, and the woman all searched diligently. This is the kind of joyous, purposeful discovery God wants us all to have in our relationship with Him. Perhaps this is why Proverbs calls the process of searching a "glory."

We can apply the same principle to our lives today. The more we believe there's something left to learn, the more likely we are to search for the truths God has to share. If we pour over His Word with purpose and desire, great are the opportunities of discovery. Like treasure buried in the earth, they've been there all along, merely waiting to be sought after. Without faith and a desire to search though, the likelihood of recovery virtually disappears. Our desire to recover the truths of God's Word is what Satan greatly fears, and why he wars so intently against it.

May we all be encouraged to maintain a healthy, childlike curiosity that always believes God for the simple but profound possibility of more.

3

GOSPEL ELEMENTS

As we examine the biblical charge to obey the gospel, it is reasonable to visit Paul's summation of what the good news is:

> Now I make known to you, brethren, the gospel which I preached to you, which also you received, in which also you stand, by which also you are saved, if you hold fast the word which I preached to you, unless you believed in vain. For I delivered to you as of first importance what I also received, that Christ died for our sins according to the Scriptures, and that He was buried, and that He was raised on the third day according to the Scriptures. (1Corinthians 15:1-4)

The gospel elements are clearly that:

- Christ died
- was buried
- rose again the third day

On a side note, it is interesting to see Paul go on in the next four verses to make six references to Jesus being *seen* after the resurrection, which we could easily call the fourth gospel element. While we don't usually include the fact that Jesus was seen post-resurrection as part of the gospel, this was definitely good news as well! (See 1Corinthans 15:5-8)

The gospel is the foundational, saving part of our faith, and understanding how to obey its message is essential. Toward this end, let's briefly look at each part of Christ's saving example.

Death

The first gospel element is Jesus' death. Thank God that Christ selflessly died to take the penalty for our sins. Obedience to His death means we must identify with it in some way. How do we participate in this initial part of the good news? The following references show that when believers identify with the death of Christ they *die to sin*:

> He Himself bore our sins in His body on the cross, so that we might die to sin and live to righteousness. (1Peter 2:24)

> May it never be! How shall we who died to sin still live in it? (Romans 6:2)

> Even so consider yourselves to be dead to sin, but alive to God in Christ Jesus. (Romans 6:11)

These scriptures answer the "what" of obeying His death, but how were believers instructed to do this? Simply put, to die to sin means to stop serving sin by walking away from it. This is simply known as repentance. Repentance is an old-fashioned word that literally means *to turn away from*, or *to change one's mind*. We repent by regretting our sins enough to stop committing them, placing our faith in Jesus Christ with a desire to live for Him in His righteousness. Simply put, Christ died *for* sins, and believers die *to* sins.

John the Baptist, Jesus, and the apostles, all emphasized repentance. Many verses refer to it and several are below. While some leaders today might not even teach repentance, it's evident this is a critical part of Christianity we must identify with as a basic part of obeying the gospel:

1. *John the Baptist preached repentance*: "John the Baptist came, preaching in the wilderness of Judea, saying, 'Repent, for the kingdom of heaven is at hand.' " (Matthew 3:1-2)

2. *Jesus preached repentance*: "From that time Jesus began to preach and say, 'Repent, for the kingdom of heaven is at hand.'" (Matthew 4:17) "I am not come to call the righteous, but sinners to repentance." (Matthew 9:13 KJV)

3. *The apostles preached repentance*: "They went out and preached that men should repent." (Mark 6:12) "Therefore repent and return, so that your sins may be wiped away." (Acts 3:19) "Therefore having overlooked the times of ignorance, God is now declaring to men that all people everywhere should repent:" (Acts 17:30) "For the sorrow that is according to the

will of God produces a repentance without regret, leading to salvation, but the sorrow of the world produces death." (2Corinthians 7:10)

This is by no means an exhaustive study of repentance, but it is clear that God wants all of us to identify with this part of the gospel by turning away from sin and toward His Lordship for our lives. Accepting the death of Christ by faith means to obey His death through our repentance. Just as Jesus' death on the cross should never be taken lightly, neither should our death to sin.

If you have not identified with Christ's death by repenting of your sins, there's no time like the present. Real repentance invests the needed time and energy to fall in love with Christ and out of love with sin and self. Repentance doesn't mean you'll live a mistake-free life; rather that you will be honest about your sinfulness and need of Christ's righteousness by refusing to serve sin as your master any longer. If you genuinely desire to identify with the gospel, begin by sincerely asking Jesus to forgive your sins and to show you how to follow His Word and will for your life.

Recognizing repentance

At least two things provide a good measure of the presence or absence of repentance in the life of a believer: how you feel when you commit sin and your subsequent response. If you're truly sorry for your sins and turn away from them and toward Christ's Lordship, it's a good indication that you've identified with the death of Christ. If, however, you love sin more than Christ and continue catering to sin's demands and the will of your flesh, you still must take the step of agreeing with Jesus' death by confessing and forsaking your sins. Real repentance means you've *died* to sin.

Psalm 51 gives a powerful example of a repentant heart. King David wrote this psalm of repentance after committing adultery with Bathsheba and arranging her husband Uriah's death so he could marry her in an attempt to hide his sin. (See 2Samuel 11, 12):

> For the choir director. A Psalm of David, when Nathan the prophet came to him, after he had gone in to Bathsheba. Be gracious to me, O God, according to Your lovingkindness; According to the greatness of Your compassion blot out my transgressions. Wash me thoroughly from my iniquity And cleanse me from my sin. For I know my transgressions, And my sin is ever before me. Against You, You only, I have sinned And done what is evil in Your sight, So that You are justified when You speak And blameless when You judge. Behold, I was brought forth in iniquity, And in sin my mother conceived me. Behold, You desire truth in the innermost being, And in the hidden part You will make me know wisdom. Purify me with hyssop, and I shall be clean; Wash me, and I shall be whiter than snow. Make me to hear joy and gladness, Let the bones which You have broken rejoice. Hide Your face from my sins And blot out all my iniquities. Create in me a clean heart, O God, And renew a steadfast spirit within me. Do not cast me away from Your presence And do not take Your Holy Spirit from me. Restore to me the joy of Your salvation And sustain me with a willing spirit. (Psalm 51:1-12)

When the prophet Nathan confronted David with the terrible nature of his sin, David didn't try to hide it, justify himself, or blame someone else for his actions. Instead, he admitted failure and his need of God's help. He mourned and pleaded with God for forgiveness, cleansing, and pardon.

In conclusion, believers can easily know how to obey the death of Christ. We do so by dying to sin through repentance.

Burial

Moving to the next part of the good news, we see that accepting and obeying the burial of Jesus by faith involves being baptized with Christ:

> Do you not know that all of us who have been baptized into Christ Jesus have been baptized into His death? Therefore we have been buried with Him through baptism into death, so that as Christ was raised from the dead through the glory of the Father, so we too might walk in newness of life. (Romans 6:3-4)

> In Him you were also circumcised with a circumcision made
> without hands, in the removal of the body of the flesh by the
> circumcision of Christ; having been buried with Him in baptism,
> in which you were also raised up with Him through faith in the
> working of God, who raised Him from the dead. (Colossians
> 2:11-12)

These verses provide powerful evidence that we are buried with Christ by faith when we follow scriptural examples of water baptism. This is so personal and intimate that the Bible states we are buried *with* Him. New Testament baptism is even compared to the covenantal relationship of Old Testament circumcision, where God now cuts away our sins so they are remembered no more.

Is baptism nothing more than an outward demonstration of an inward faith? In one sense, baptism indeed demonstrates our obedience by faith, but a closer look shows it is where God has chosen to impart so much more to us. Consider what Jesus said happens at baptism:

> And He said to them, "Go into all the world and preach the
> gospel to all creation. He who has believed and has been
> baptized shall be saved; but he who has disbelieved shall be
> condemned." (Mark 16:15-16)

In this passage, we see Jesus establish a powerful connection between baptism and salvation from sin. Did Jesus say, "He that believes is saved, and then should be baptized?" No, He did not say that salvation comes when we believe and baptism is apart from it. Rather He said that both believing the gospel and being baptized are a part of salvation. This answer agrees perfectly with Colossians 2:11-12 above, which shows that God has chosen our baptism to "put off" the body of sins.

Peter also cited baptism as a part of God's saving grace when he compared it to the saving of Noah and eight of his family members in the ark:

> For Christ also died for sins once for all, the just for the unjust,
> so that He might bring us to God, having been put to death in
> the flesh, but made alive in the spirit; in which also He went
> and made proclamation to the spirits now in prison, who once

were disobedient, when the patience of God kept waiting in the days of Noah . . . in which a few, that is, eight persons, were brought safely through the water. Corresponding to that, baptism now saves you—not the removal of dirt from the flesh, but an appeal to God for a good conscience—through the resurrection of Jesus Christ. (1Peter 3:18-21)

As I grew up in church, we were not taught about this scriptural connection between partaking in the burial of Christ at baptism and His cutting away of sins. Learning about this was very good news and revealed a very powerful truth from God's word I was happy to apply.

Baptism and the blood: The blood is applied in the water

Many will say that water cannot wash away our sins, and that is certainly correct. There is obviously no inherent power in water to cleanse sins; the blood of Christ is the only thing that can wash them away. However, God has clearly connected water baptism and the *application* of the blood of His Son to the believer. This is why Christ said what He did in Mark 16 about believing the gospel and identifying with His burial—that it saves us from our sins. We will see more about this connection as we continue to examine what the Bible says about this subject.

In another passage, Christ stated something to His disciples that has puzzled many believers:

> If you forgive the sins of any, their sins have been forgiven them; if you retain the sins of any, they have been retained. (John 20:23)

First, let's think about what Jesus did not say. He was not giving the apostles the authority to forgive people's sins by their own power—that belonged to Him alone. He did not mean they could choose to whom they would extend the invitation to receive forgiveness, because elsewhere Christ said whoever wanted to could come to Him. However, Jesus *was* giving the apostles a commission to minister to people, and when they administered baptism, the believers' sins were washed away. Conversely, if the people refused to believe and be baptized, their sins would be retained. Only the blood of Christ has the power to wash away sins, and the Lord has ordained that His saving blood be applied to believers in the waters of baptism.

We see further evidence of this connection when John wrote:

> This is the One who came by water and blood, Jesus Christ; not with the water only, but with the water and with the blood. It is the Spirit who testifies, because the Spirit is the truth. For there are three that testify: the Spirit and the water and the blood; and the three are in agreement. (1John 5:6-8)

By God's grace, the Spirit, the water, and the blood agree. The testimony of their agreement was authored at Calvary's cross, and is accessed by believers at baptism. This is where the agreement takes place in the life of a believer. As to how the Spirit agrees with the water and the blood, we will see later that those who receive New Testament baptism also receive the promise of being filled with the Holy Spirit—further evidencing this scriptural agreement.

In yet another example, Saul's baptism provides an additional witness that sins are washed by Jesus' blood when Ananias said to him, "Now why do you delay? Get up and be baptized, and wash away your sins, calling on His name." (Acts 22:16) It is interesting to note, even though Saul had already repented and placed his faith in Christ at this point, Ananias understood his sins still needed to be washed away by Jesus' blood, which would be accomplished at baptism according to this passage.

The understanding that Jesus' blood is applied to our sinful lives at baptism took some getting used to, as my denomination did not teach me this. Moreover, I know that many others might not agree with this position. To help my own search, I asked the simple but fair question; "If Jesus' saving blood *isn't* applied to believers at baptism, then when is it applied by faith?" I had to admit, the scriptures did present a clear and consistent connection of the two. There is still more evidence we have yet to study, including many actual instances of souls being saved from sin. The precedent of their examples will prove very helpful to our investigation.

Putting on Christ

Interestingly, Scripture also reveals that baptism is how we use our faith to "put on" or "clothe" ourselves with Christ. In baptism with Him, He also claims us as His possession, we become one with Him and heirs:

> For you are all sons of God through faith in Christ Jesus. For all of you who were baptized into Christ have clothed yourselves with Christ. . . . you are all one in Christ Jesus. And if you belong to Christ, then you are Abraham's descendants, heirs according to promise. (Galatians 3:26-29)

According to these verses, the benefits to being buried with Christ at baptism reach far beyond a mere outward demonstration of an inward faith. It is eye opening to see that Jesus actually clothes our sinfulness with His innocence as we are "buried" in this watery grave with Him by faith.

Baptismal method—is it important?

We've seen why baptism is important. Let's examine if *how* we are baptized is important. Since God has chosen to impart so much of His saving grace at our obedience to this command, it would be reasonable to make sure we apply it consistently with biblical examples. Baptism is administered in different ways today, but Paul said in Ephesians 4:5 that there is only "one Lord, one faith, one baptism." If we take the time to investigate, we can easily discover and follow the scriptural pattern.

Through the first centuries of church history and according to the biblical accounts, there was in fact only one consistent method of baptism for gospel believers. If baptism is as important as Scripture reveals, then we should know all we can about it. Sometimes the subject becomes clearer when we learn words or phrases from the original language in which they were expressed. This calls for some definitions of the Greek words for baptism:

> G907 baptizō From a derivative of G911; to *make whelmed* (that is, *fully wet*); used only (in the New Testament) of ceremonial *ablution*, especially (technically) of the ordinance of Christian *baptism:*—baptist, baptize, wash.

> G911 baptō A primary verb; to *whelm*, that is, cover wholly with a fluid; in the New Testament only in a qualified or specific sense, that is, (literally) to *moisten* (a part of one's person), or (by implication) to *stain* (as with dye): —dip.

These definitions support the fact that baptism is indeed a "burial" with Christ. When someone is buried in a mausoleum or in the earth, there is always complete covering. This total enclosing provides the needed protection for the deceased. As a young believer, I was never encouraged to understand these subjects, so I never knew that to be baptized literally meant to be covered completely with water. Only later through careful study did I learn that I hadn't been baptized according to the biblical precedent, nor was the invocation given over me consistent with scriptural examples. When I discovered and obeyed the burial of Christ to follow the biblical method, it was an unforgettable and life-changing experience.

Sprinkling

As stated above, the verb "baptizo" means "to whelm" (immerse), but "sprinkle" is the Greek verb "rhantizo." Interestingly, these words are never used interchangeably in any Bible examples of baptism, as they have separate and distinct meanings. If sprinkling were equivalent to immersing, we would definitely notice this in Scripture:

> G4472 rhantizō From a derivative of rhain ō (to *sprinkle*); to *render besprinkled*, that is, *asperse* (ceremonially or figuratively): - sprinkle.

If we can find no scriptural evidence where rhantizo (sprinkling) is used in the Bible, then how could anyone think it is the same thing as baptizo/baptism, or that it doesn't matter which method is used? This question certainly does not imply that people who were sprinkled were not sincere. I'm only stating that we should be careful to thoroughly obey what Scripture commands. If biblical precedents are set aside in favor of one's own preferences, where would it stop?

At about eleven years of age, I remember being disappointed when I was sprinkled in a church ceremony. I wondered, "Where is the change? Isn't something supposed to happen?" Oh, but the difference was unmistakable when I was baptized according to the biblical pattern! There was simply no comparison. I'm so glad I didn't settle for less than what God's Word had for me.

Resurrection

We've seen that believers can obey the death and burial of Christ by dying to sin at repentance and through being buried with Him at baptism. The next step of God's grace-imparting good news is the supernatural resurrection of Jesus from the grave.

"Obey Christ's resurrection—how can we use faith to do what seems to be humanly impossible?" Rest assured that the Bible accounts will clearly reveal how believers accept this part of the good news into their lives also.

First, it's important to acknowledge there will be an absolutely supernatural resurrection of the dead at the return of Christ for His church. According to 1Thessalonians 4:16-17, those who are ready, both alive and dead, will be caught up to meet Christ in the air. This will obviously identify them with His resurrection. However, by the time this event happens, believers must have *already* believed and obeyed the gospel message to be ready for that great day. Therefore, the question remains; how did Bible converts initially identify with Jesus' resurrection as a normal part of obeying the gospel?

The big "if"

Romans 8:9-11 shows us that if the same Spirit that raised Jesus from the dead dwells in us, it will be the source of our resurrection. Soberly, verse 9 informs us this is so important that if we do not have this Spirit, we do not even belong to Jesus. That's a very big "if." Before the Second Coming, we must receive His resurrecting Spirit if we want to be His. This passage does not record anyone receiving the Spirit, it merely points to this necessity. We will see how believers received His Spirit in a later chapter. For now, we can know the way to obey Christ's resurrection is to have the same Spirit that raised Jesus from the dead living in us:

> However, you are not in the flesh but in the Spirit, if indeed the Spirit of God dwells in you. But if anyone does not have the Spirit of Christ, he does not belong to Him. If Christ is in you, though the body is dead because of sin, yet the spirit is alive because of righteousness. But if the Spirit of Him who raised Jesus from the dead dwells in you, He who raised Christ Jesus from the dead will also give life to your mortal bodies through His Spirit who dwells in you. (Romans 8:9-11)

This reading reveals another powerful truth. A careful examination indicates the Spirit of God is the same as the Spirit of Christ, and is in fact Christ in you. It is so important that we receive Christ by faith into our lives to be part of Him, and we definitely do so by receiving His Spirit. Ephesians also confirms this wonderful fact:

> that He would grant you, according to the riches of His glory, to be strengthened with power through His Spirit in the inner man, so that Christ may dwell in your hearts through faith; (Ephesians 3:16-17)

In John 14, Jesus also agrees perfectly with Romans 8. The Spirit, which He calls the Comforter, will in fact be Himself dwelling in us. Again, we see that to receive the Spirit of God is to receive Jesus Christ:

> And I will pray the Father, and he shall give you another Comforter, that he may abide with you for ever; Even the Spirit of truth; whom the world cannot receive, because it seeth him not, neither knoweth him: but ye know him; for he dwelleth with

you, and shall be in you. I will not leave you comfortless: I will come to you. (John 14:16-18 KJV)

First Corinthians further illustrates that being baptized by God's Spirit is what actually puts us "into" the body of Christ: "For by one Spirit we were all baptized into one body . . . and we were all made to drink of one Spirit." (1Corinthians 12:13)

Many more passages refer to the importance of believers receiving the Spirit of Christ. In Acts 5, we see a direct connection of obedience and receiving the Holy Spirit. Luke then records Jesus' teaching of the importance of asking to receive the Holy Spirit. (See Acts 5:32, Luke 11:13)

All of these witnesses and more show many of the reasons Jesus wants to fill all believers with His Spirit. The blessings and benefits of being filled are so many that we don't have the space to explore them here.[2]

When do believers receive the Spirit?

Since receiving the Holy Spirit is so important, it is reasonable to know the answers to the following questions: How do we know we've received His Spirit? Where are the biblical examples of others receiving it? Has God changed His method of filling believers with the Holy Spirit? Do we automatically have it when we place our faith in Christ? Personal opinions are of little value, so we must allow the Bible to provide the answers. Don't be troubled if you see something different from what you have been taught, or maybe even from what you teach others. Seeing that

---

[2] Here's a partial list of what receiving the Spirit will do: guide us into all truth (John 16:13); set us free from the law of sin and death (Rom 8:2); make us partakers of the righteousness, peace, and joy of God's kingdom (Rom 14:17); teach us (1Co 2:13); wash, sanctify and justify us (1Co 6:11); place us into the body of Christ (1Co 12:13); give us the blessing of Abraham (Gal 3:14); make us heirs of God (Gal 4:6-7); grant us access to the Father (Eph 2:18); strengthen our inner man and allow Christ to dwell in us by faith (Eph 3:16-17) .

God has more for us is a good thing, and an opportunity to continue receiving more from Him:

> In Him, you also, after listening to the message of truth, the gospel of your salvation—having also believed, you were sealed in Him with the Holy Spirit of promise. (Ephesians 1:13)

In this passage, the hearers placed faith in Jesus when they heard the gospel, and it was sometime *after* they believed that they were sealed with the Spirit, not *when* they believed. This doesn't agree with what is often taught today; that believers automatically have the Spirit at the point of belief. This doesn't mean that people can't be filled at the point of belief, because it happens in a scriptural example we will see. While it can happen both ways, we will see that both belief and obedience are present when the believers receive the Spirit.

Acts 8 offers another example that plainly shows believers are not necessarily filled with God's Spirit at the moment of faith in Christ, or even when they are baptized. When the Samaritans placed their faith in Jesus, they repented of trusting in sorceries and they were baptized, but they hadn't yet been filled with the Holy Spirit. It was only afterward that they received it. (See Acts 8:14-17)

The Samaritans' experience shows that receiving the Holy Spirit doesn't necessarily happen at the point of belief.[3] This prompts us to dig into the Bible further to understand exactly when we receive the Spirit, especially as we've seen how indispensable it is to our salvation.

If believers don't automatically have the Spirit of Christ the moment they believe in Christ, then when do they receive it? How can they know they have received it? Jesus gave us an important insight into these questions when He addressed Nicodemus in John 3.

---

[3] See also Acts 19:1-6.

Jesus' profound teaching of John 3:8

In John 3:8 Jesus delivered a vital though often overlooked teaching when He compared being born of the Spirit with hearing the wind. He unmistakably stated there would be a "sound" associated with *everyone* who is born of the Spirit. He didn't explain what that sound was there, but we'll discover exactly what it is when we see the biblical accounts of those who are actually receiving the Spirit:

> "The wind blows where it wishes and you hear the sound of it, but do not know where it comes from and where it is going; so is everyone who is born of the Spirit." (John 3:8)

Conclusions

Throughout my formative years in church, I don't remember being taught anything about receiving God's Spirit. After I received it and learned how important it was, I experienced very mixed emotions. These ranged from elation and joy at the grace of God that allowed such a definite infilling, to being upset that it had been kept from me, even though I was a believer and faithful churchgoer for many years.

It might come as a shock, but you may find through Bible examination (as I did) that you are not yet filled with God's Spirit. If you see this through your studies, know that God wants you to have it, and that discovering more truth from Scripture is a normal part of God's ongoing plan to guide us. Not only does He want you to receive it, He wants to give it to you exactly as His Word shows. When I received the Spirit, it was the most awesome thing I had ever experienced. I didn't have to speculate if I received it or not. I was able to go to the Bible and verify it by other examples. We do not have to settle for less proof today.

I also discovered that my Holy Spirit infilling was not an isolated experience, but God was doing the same thing all over the world for millions of people with open hearts. If you are wondering, "Will

God do it for me?" be assured that He not only wants to, but He has promised that if you will respond with simple obedience to the gospel message, He will fill you. We'll explore more about this specific promise in detail later.

As we move further into our study, you might see a very different way of responding to the good news than you've understood to date. If this is the case, don't be afraid to demonstrate newfound faith by responding again to the gospel. If you see something new or different in the Bible, try not to think of it as new, but merely new to you. If it's in God's Word, it's an old and good path:

> Thus says the LORD, "Stand by the ways and see and ask for the ancient paths, Where the good way is, and walk in it; And you will find rest for your souls." But they said, "We will not walk in it." (Jeremiah 6:16)

Here the Lord was trying to restore something good and restful to His people. Sadly, they refused. Our generation will also forfeit wonderful blessings if we reject God's attempts to restore His Word to us.

We've identified the connection of Christ's death to our repentance, His burial with our baptism, and His resurrection to receiving His Spirit. We see just how comprehensive this theme is as we move through the New Testament, continuing with John the Baptist and Jesus Christ.

4

JOHN THE BAPTIST AND JESUS TAUGHT OBEDIENCE TO THE GOSPEL

John the Baptist

It should come as no shock that John the Baptist also reveals the pattern of obeying the gospel. According to Isaiah and Matthew, John's mission was to teach people to "prepare the way of the Lord" and to "make His paths straight." How do we follow John's instructions, and why does the Lord need us to make a path for Him? Can't He navigate wherever He wants? Of course, but there is one place He can't go without our cooperation, and that's into our hearts. We hold the key of acceptance or rejection of His Lordship in our lives. As the old saying goes, the Lord is a gentleman, and will only go where invited.

What John proclaimed completely agrees with the blueprint of identifying with the death, burial, and resurrection identified in the previous chapter. In Matthew 3:1-11 John tucked these gospel elements into his teaching by pointing people to the Messiah:

> *John first called for people to repent.* "Repent, for the kingdom of heaven is at hand." (Matthew3:2)

> *Next, believers demonstrated their faith in John's message by being baptized.* "Then Jerusalem was going out to him, and all Judea and all the district around the Jordan; and they were being baptized by him in the Jordan River, as they confessed their sins." (Matthew 3:5-6)

Why was this so important? What did obeying this instruction accomplish? Mark wrote that baptism is for *forgiveness* or *remission* of sins. "John the Baptist appeared in the wilderness preaching a baptism of repentance for the forgiveness of sins." (Mark 1:4)

> Forgiveness: (Greek G859 aphesis *af'-es-is* From G863; *freedom*; [figuratively] *pardon:* - deliverance, forgiveness, liberty, remission)

As we have seen, this is when the blood of Christ would be applied to believers by faith. Even though Jesus hadn't yet shed His blood on the cross during John's ministry, John was preparing His way.

God has chosen to apply His sin-cleansing blood as we demonstrate our faith through this simple act of obedience. He could have chosen anything, but He chose baptism. One reason could have been that for many years Jews baptized Gentile proselytes as a symbol of having their old lives washed away as they entered into covenant with Jehovah. Whether this was His reason or not, it is tremendous to see how and why obeying this part of the good news is so beneficial.

> *John then pointed believers to Jesus, who would baptize them with the Holy Spirit and fire.* "I baptize you with water for repentance, but He who is coming after me is mightier than I. . . He will baptize you with the Holy Spirit and fire." (Matthew 3:11)

Instead of external Jewish ritual and law, in His New Covenant, God's Holy Spirit would actually dwell within the hearts of men and they would become members of a spiritual kingdom. This without question would be the greatest gift humanity had ever known. John prepared the way for New Testament believers to gain access to the greatest message of history, the gospel of Christ's death, burial, and resurrection.

In conclusion, we see John's ministry instructing believers to:

1. Turn away from sin in *repentance*
2. Be *baptized* in water for the forgiveness of sins
3. Expect to be baptized with God's *Holy Spirit*

John's message was in one hundred percent agreement with the biblical pattern of obeying the gospel: death/repentance, burial/baptism, resurrection/receiving the Holy Spirit of Christ.

John's message prepared listeners for Christ's Lordship, and it was a perfect foreshadowing of receiving the good news.

Jesus continued the same model

It is no coincidence that Jesus also preached the same message of repentance, baptism, and the coming infilling of His Spirit:

Repentance

> From that time Jesus began to preach and say, "Repent, for the kingdom of heaven is at hand." (Matthew 4:17)

> Jesus came into Galilee, preaching the gospel of God and saying, "The time is fulfilled, and the kingdom of God is at hand; repent and believe in the gospel." (Mark 1:14-15)

> "Unless you repent, you will all likewise perish." (Luke 13:3)

Baptism

Jesus personally demonstrated one way of fulfilling righteousness by being baptized in Matthew 3 (See also Mark 1:9, Luke 3:21) and by having His followers baptized in John 3 and 4:

> Then Jesus arrived from Galilee at the Jordan coming to John, to be baptized by him. But John tried to prevent Him, saying, "I have need to be baptized by You, and do You come to me?" But Jesus answering said to him, "Permit it at this time; for in this way it is fitting for us to fulfill all righteousness." Then he permitted Him. After being baptized, Jesus came up immediately from the water; and behold, the heavens were opened, and he saw the Spirit of God descending as a dove and lighting on Him, and behold, a voice out of the heavens said, "This is My beloved Son, in whom I am well-pleased." (Matthew 3:13-17)

> After these things Jesus and His disciples came into the land of Judea, and there He was spending time with them and baptizing. (John 3:22)

> Therefore when the Lord knew that the Pharisees had heard that Jesus was making and baptizing more disciples than John

(although Jesus Himself was not baptizing, but His disciples were). (John 4:1-2)

Notice in the accounts of Christ's baptism (Matthew 3:16, Mark 1:10, Luke 3:21-22) that the Spirit descended upon Jesus as a direct result of obeying God's mandate of baptism, along with the supernatural presence and voice of God speaking. This provides an interesting connection with what Jesus referred to in John 3:8; about there being a sound associated with everyone that is born of the Spirit, and as we will later see, how New Testament baptism is connected with a promise of receiving God's Spirit.

> Immediately coming up out of the water, He saw the heavens opening, and the Spirit like a dove descending upon Him; and a voice came out of the heavens: "You are My beloved Son, in You I am well-pleased." (Mark 1:10)

> Now when all the people were baptized, Jesus was also baptized, and while He was praying, heaven was opened, The Holy Spirit descended upon Him in bodily form like a dove, and a voice came out of heaven, "You are My beloved Son, in You I am well-pleased." (Luke 3:21-22)

Holy Spirit

In John 7, Jesus foretold of the day when believers could and would receive the Holy Spirit, and that this was supposed to happen for all believers—but they had to thirst for it. This further evidences Christ's preparation of believers to identify with His resurrection:

> On the last day, the great day of the feast, Jesus stood and cried out, saying, "If anyone is thirsty, let him come to Me and drink. He who believes in Me, as the Scripture said, 'From his innermost being will flow rivers of living water.' " But this He spoke of the Spirit, whom those who believed in Him were to receive; for the Spirit was not yet given, because Jesus was not yet glorified. (John 7:37-39)[4]

---

[4] Jesus also referred to the coming infilling of His Holy Spirit in John 4:14 when He spoke to the Samaritan woman at the well about giving her "living water" if

In Luke 11:13 Jesus said, "If you then, being evil, know how to give good gifts to your children: how much more will your heavenly Father give the Holy Spirit to those that ask him?" Despite going to church for years, I never knew that I needed to *ask* the Lord to give me His Holy Spirit. I sure am glad I did. What an awesome, empowering difference it has made.

Conclusions

Unmistakably, John the Baptist and Jesus were on the same page with their message that prepared believers to receive the kingdom of God. While Jesus obviously taught about many subjects, we can see from these passages a consistent message pointing us toward preparing the Lord's pathway into our lives through repentance, baptism, and the infilling of God's Holy Spirit. With study, it becomes clear that this is how believers obey and identify with the death, burial, and resurrection of Christ. We will notice a complete harmony and agreement with this pattern when we read the post-resurrection conversion accounts in the following chapter.

---

she would ask, and to Nicodemus in John 3 when He referred to the requirement of being born again of water and Spirit.

5

THE GREAT COMMISSION
AND OBEYING THE GOSPEL

One of the most powerful truths about Scripture is how all its books and themes agree. This proves to be no different in its various perspectives of applying the gospel. We've seen this message move throughout the epistles, to John the Baptist and to Jesus. Now we will see the torch given to the apostles.

Just before Jesus ascended to Heaven, He gave His disciples their last instructions. We call these weighty commands the Great Commission. When we compare what Jesus said to what these men did, we'll notice a clear and unbroken connection to the emerging pattern of obeying the gospel as Christ's plan for accepting His Lordship and salvation.

The Great Commission in Matthew:

> And Jesus came up and spoke to them, saying, "All authority has been given to Me in heaven and on earth. Go therefore and make disciples of all the nations, baptizing them in the name of the Father and the Son and the Holy Spirit, teaching them to observe all that I commanded you; and lo, I am with you always, even to the end of the age." (Matthew 28:18-20)

Mark's version:

> And He [Jesus] said to them, "Go into all the world and preach the gospel to all creation. He who has believed and has been baptized shall be saved; but he who has disbelieved shall be condemned. These signs will accompany those who have believed: in My name they will cast out demons, they will speak with new tongues; they will pick up serpents, and if they drink any deadly *poison,* it will not hurt them; they will lay hands on the sick, and they will recover." (Mark 16:15-18)

Luke's continues by recording:

> And said unto them, Thus it is written, and thus it behooved Christ to suffer, and to rise from the dead the third day: And that repentance and remission of sins should be preached in his name among all nations, beginning at Jerusalem. (Luke 24:46-47 KJV)

A quick synopsis of these commandments shows Jesus instructed the apostles to:

1. Make disciples of all nations, baptizing them in the name of the Father, and of the Son, and of the Holy Spirit
2. Teach them to observe everything Jesus has commanded them
3. Preach the gospel to every creature, baptizing those who believe, with expectation of signs following
4. Preach repentance and remission of sins among all nations, specifically in Christ's name

Accepting Jesus Christ as Lord

Many if not most churches today teach that people must come to God by accepting Jesus Christ as their Lord and personal Savior. This is absolutely essential, for there is no other pathway to salvation than through His Lordship in our lives.

In practice, a leader usually says a prayer for the hearers to repeat, they pray for acceptance and conclude by asking Jesus to come into their hearts. Then the speaker might say that those who repeated the prayer are now saved, or born again and ready for Heaven. The procedure and wording may vary, but this method is widely used by many believing groups today.

Since this is an eternally significant step, it's reasonable that we should be able to thoroughly and biblically address the following:

> · If accepting Christ in this way is the pattern we are supposed to follow to access the work of His cross and empty tomb, we should be able to show any new believer specific instances in the Bible where people accepted Christ in this manner.

- As believers or believing leaders, we should be able to confirm for ourselves if this was how conversions consistently happened in scriptural accounts of believers coming to Christ for salvation.

Weighty questions

The following questions go to the heart of what is most important in life and eternity—receiving the salvation of Jesus Christ into our lives. As you consider these potentially uncomfortable questions, please think of the exercise as a reasonable examination that can only confirm what is true about our beliefs:

- Is it appropriate to present methods of applying the gospel that differ from biblical examples?

- What should we do if the Bible shows new believers obeying the gospel differently than you or I instruct them to currently?

- Is it acceptable to use Scripture passages that reference the *concept* of salvation as the *pattern* of receiving the good news when no one is actually responding to the gospel in the verses?

- If Scripture never shows new believers being led through a sinner's prayer or similar method of accepting Christ, could it be that God is trying to restore faithfulness to the biblical pattern of applying the gospel?

Depending on the answers to these questions, many may see the need to adjust the way they lead people to respond to the gospel so their practice agrees with biblical accounts. This may sound radical or revolutionary, but when we boil it down, changing one's mind and methods to agree with Scripture should be normal as God continues to reveal more of His Word to us. The Lord values this kind of honest examination born out of a hunger for truth, and will be faithful through every step of our journey with Him. If He brings you to a positive change like this, He will definitely see you through it.

Cause for celebration

As we search the Scriptures, when we discover something we previously didn't see, it's definitely a reason to rejoice. Like the man who discovered the pearl of great price, the shepherd who located his lost sheep or the woman who found her lost coin, discoveries should inspire celebration. On the occasions that God convicts us to act anew upon His Word, it shouldn't be a reason to become defensive or upset. If He takes the time to show us something, this is only further proof of His love for us and leadership in our lives—and all the more reason to happily receive it.

These examples share a common thread; they all demonstrate people searching for something. The individuals were motivated to find what was lost, or to find something more valuable than what they had already discovered. The pearl, the coin, and sheep didn't spring up into the surprised arms of the discoverer; they were sought after. When found, it was only right to celebrate.

As Solomon admonished his son to search for wisdom in Proverbs 4, may we always search the Scriptures to confirm the practices we believe to be true. If we find more than we've known before, let us honor the occasion by demonstrating our faith with gratitude and simple obedience, even if it means responding again to something we've already believed. Our continued discoveries of the valuable truths of God's Word should be as the unearthing of a priceless treasure—even if we've been walking with Him for a long time, and the treasure hasn't been in our family for generations.

So how do we know if we've obeyed the gospel of Christ completely? We can't merely rely on the concept of being "saved" as the pattern. The only way is to trust the Bible by honestly measuring ourselves by its examples of others doing so. As we do, we'll see the complete connection between the Great Commission and how the apostles led new believers to accept Jesus through applying each part of the saving gospel by faith.

Receiving the grace of Christ through the gospel

All we have studied to this point brings us to see how post-resurrection believers responded to the gospel. How they applied the death, burial, and resurrection of Christ will give us the template we must also follow. Their examples will clearly reveal the consistent plan for the New Testament.

The first place we see the gospel preached is shortly after Jesus' ascension to Heaven early in the Book of Acts. Jesus had predicted the apostles would soon be filled with the Holy Spirit, thus identifying with His victorious resurrection. "Gathering them together, He [Jesus] commanded them not to leave Jerusalem, but to wait for what the Father had promised, 'Which,' He said, 'you heard of from Me; for John baptized with water, but you will be baptized with the Holy Spirit not many days from now.'" (Acts 1:4-5) Peter would preach the inaugural gospel message of the church soon after this promised infilling.

Early in Acts 2, the apostles, Mary the mother of Jesus, and over one hundred others were wonderfully filled with the Holy Spirit. This first instance of infilling is commonly referred to as the birth of the church:

> When the day of Pentecost had come, they were all together in one place. And suddenly there came from heaven a noise like a violent rushing wind, and it filled the whole house where they were sitting. And there appeared to them tongues as of fire distributing themselves, and they rested on each one of them. And they were all filled with the Holy Spirit and began to speak with other tongues, as the Spirit was giving them utterance. (Acts 2:1-4)

Notice that when they were receiving the Holy Spirit, they spoke the deeds of God in languages they had not learned. Bystanders from many different countries were astonished when they understood these Jews, as they spoke in their own native tongues. (See Acts 2:6-11)

This precedent is very important because it is the first example of the "sound" heard when post-resurrection believers are born of the

Spirit. If we can see a consistent pattern when people are Spirit-filled, we'll be able to identify the sound Jesus predicted would accompany this infilling. Jesus could have said in John 3:8 that we'd *feel* the wind blow when someone is born of the Spirit, or we would *see* where the wind blows, but He didn't. He purposefully said that we would *hear* a sound:

> The wind blows where it wishes and you hear the sound of it, but do not know where it comes from and where it is going; so is everyone who is born of the Spirit. (John 3:8)

In Acts 2, as people were born of the Spirit, they all spoke with other languages. It is also interesting to note; just as Jesus' resurrection was a supernatural result of the Spirit entering the dead body of Christ, obeying the resurrection for these believers is evidenced by a supernatural work of the Spirit as it entered them—after they have first experienced their own personal death to sin at repentance. We saw Jesus address this topic in Mark 16:17 where He said that speaking with new languages/tongues would be a normal happening for believers.

Even though I was never taught I could have this infilling while growing up, I experienced it in exactly the same way as described in Acts 2. I was so encouraged to see the connection between what Jesus predicted and promised in the gospels with what the apostles and the believers experienced in the Bible. Receiving the Holy Spirit was definitely the greatest thing that ever happened in my life.

Not only did Jesus predict the infilling of the Holy Spirit, the prophet Isaiah foretold it hundreds of years before it happened:

> To whom would He teach knowledge, And to whom would He interpret the message? . . . For *He says,* 'Order on order, order on order, Line on line, line on line, A little here, a little there.' Indeed, He will speak to this people through stammering lips and a foreign tongue, He who said to them, 'Here is rest, give rest to the weary,' And, 'Here is repose,' but they would not listen. (Isaiah 28:9-12)

To say my experience was restful would be an enormous understatement. What the prophet seems to regret though, is that there would be individuals who wouldn't hear and receive this God-given promise Jesus would die for us to have.

I know there are many sincere believers who haven't been filled in this way yet. I was one of them. If you haven't experienced this infilling, it might be difficult to figure out how you can receive it. Acts 2:4 lets us know that it is God who gives the utterance (ability to speak), so it isn't something we have to figure out on our own. If it were, we could remove God from the process.

When I received the Holy Spirit, I absolutely spoke with a language I had not learned. Nobody coached me or told me what to say. The thing I remember most was that it happened very easily in His presence as I yielded myself to His Spirit. If you are thirsty for this well of living water, we'll soon explore exactly how you can obtain the promise of receiving the Spirit, which God wants us all to have.

Acts 2 was only the first example, though. We will see that this is consistent with other instances and not just a one-time occurrence.

When the inaugural infilling in Acts 2 happened, God poured out His Spirit so powerfully that it drew the attention of a throng of Jews who were at Jerusalem for the Feast of Pentecost. Having been given the keys to the kingdom by Christ in Matthew 16, Peter stood up with the other apostles and preached the gospel message to all who would hear him. He spoke of Jesus who had performed many miraculous things, but according to God's plan, the Jews delivered to be tried, scourged, and killed—but God raised Him from the dead. (See Acts 2:22-24)

As Peter preached, many in the crowd were convicted of causing the death of their Messiah, and they anxiously asked Peter how they should respond to the gospel message.

First response to the gospel

The next moment was history's most significant precedent for humanity because of what Jesus did on the cross and at the tomb. His death, burial, and resurrection provided access to salvation for all, and their response to the gospel is going to be our example of how to apply its saving power. If the devil ever wanted to stop us from doing anything, he would be intent on stopping us from having the faith to embrace this life-giving message.

Would the hearers accept what Peter had to say? How would these convicted souls demonstrate their saving faith? If what we have seen from the Bible so far is true, Peter must direct these souls to obey the gospel. Let's see if Peter's instructions are in agreement with the Great Commission and the pattern for which John and Jesus laid the groundwork:

> Peter said to them, "Repent, and each of you be baptized in the name of Jesus Christ for the forgiveness of your sins; and you will receive the gift of the Holy Spirit." (Acts 2:38)

Does this match what we've seen so far about obeying the death, burial, and resurrection of Christ? Does it match what both John and Jesus said? Yes, it does:

> 1. Turn away from sin in repentance (death)
> 2. Be baptized in water for the forgiveness of sins (burial)
> 3. Receive the Holy Spirit (resurrection)

Peter's instructions in verse 38 absolutely fulfilled these gospel components, and he further revealed that the promise of receiving the Holy Spirit was for everyone:

> For the promise is for you and your children and for all who are far off, as many as the Lord our God will call to Himself. And with many other words he [Peter] solemnly testified and kept on exhorting them, saying, "Be saved from this perverse generation!" (Acts 2:39-40)

You may ask, "How can I receive this promise too?" The answer is simply to obey the instructions in verse 38. Applying Christ's death and burial as prescribed grants us access to this promised, saving gift from God. He will never forget His promises and can't wait to fill believers who are hungry and thirsty for His Spirit.

In verse 40, Peter said that responding as he had directed would save the hearers. This is another example of receiving the saving power of Jesus' blood over sins by obeying Christ's burial at baptism. If this is what the first gospel-responders did to receive salvation from their sins, this is what we must also do today.

Did Peter fulfill the Great Commission?

In my formative years as a believer, I never looked into this subject, so the following was a real revelation to me, even though it was in the Bible all along. You might find yourself in a similar situation. Before we come to any conclusions, we're going to carefully examine if Peter obeyed the Great Commission on the Day of Pentecost.

The Commission instructions included preaching the gospel, teaching and baptizing all nations in the name of the Father, and the Son, and the Holy Spirit and preaching the message of repentance and remission of sins in Christ's name. Let's see if Peter fulfilled these instructions:

Did Peter preach the gospel and baptize the believers? Yes, for "Those who had received his word were baptized." (Acts 2:41)

Did Peter preach repentance and remission of sins in Christ's name? Yes he did, baptizing three thousand souls for the remission of their sins—in the name of Jesus Christ.

Did Peter baptize believers in the name of the Father and the Son and the Holy Spirit, though? There seems to be a big inconsistency in what Jesus commanded and what Peter actually did. Hadn't Peter been paying attention when Jesus spoke in Matthew 28:19? If Peter was listening to Jesus, then why did he tell the people on the Day of Pentecost to be baptized in the name of Jesus Christ? *It looks like Peter disobeyed the Great Commission.* There has to be an explanation, or else Peter misled thousands of people and they failed to respond to the gospel as Christ wanted them to.

Consider this possibility: does Peter understand something that might not be obvious at first to us? Did Peter, when he baptized so many people in Jesus' name, somehow fulfill what Jesus had commanded in Matthew 28:19? This requires careful examination, especially when it involves something as important as salvation from our sins. Since there is such emphasis on "name" in the Commission scriptures, it is reasonable to explore the following questions to begin our search for the answer:

· *What is the name of the Father?* (Does the Father even have a name other than "Father"?)
· *What is the name of the Son?* (Does the Son have a name?)
· *What is the name of the Holy Spirit?* (Does the Holy Spirit have a name?)

Some answers come easier than others do, but with some digging, we can conclusively find out the reason for this apparent contradiction.

The name of the Son

Let's start with the obvious question: what is the name of the Son of God? Without a doubt, it is Jesus Christ. (See Matthew 1:21; Mark 1:1, Luke 1:31-32)

Did Peter baptize in the name of the Son when he baptized converts in Jesus' name? Yes, he did. While it may not be obvious at first, he actually obeyed the command to baptize in the name of the Son.

The name of the Father

The answer to this point is not as obvious. What can we find out about the name of the Father? Several times Jesus provided the answer, and we can understand it in a well-known prophecy of Isaiah. Jesus plainly said that the Father *does* have a name. Some initial proof is found in the Lord's Prayer:

> Pray, then, in this way: 'Our Father who is in heaven, Hallowed be Your name.' (Matthew 6:9)

Next, Jesus revealed something interesting about His name. Even though Jesus Christ is the name of God's Son, He said He hadn't come in His own name, but in the name of His Father:

> I have come in My Father's name, and you do not receive Me; if another comes in his own name, you will receive him. (John 5:43)

This also agrees with Hebrews 1:4: "Having become as much better than the angels, as He [Jesus] has inherited a more excellent name than they."

Here is a powerful portion of scripture that directly relates to the question at hand. Look carefully in John 17 at whose name Jesus says He has manifested to his disciples—the name of His Father. This provides undeniable proof that the name of the Father is in fact the same name given to His Son:

> Now, Father, glorify Me together with Yourself, with the glory which I had with You before the world was. I have manifested Your name to the men whom You gave Me out of the world; they were Yours and You gave them to Me, and they have kept Your word. (John 17:5-6)
>
> I am no longer in the world; and yet they themselves are in the world, and I come to You. Holy Father, keep them in Your name, the name which You have given Me, that they may be one even as We are. While I was with them, I was keeping them in Your name which You have given Me; and I guarded them and not one of them perished but the son of perdition, so that the Scripture would be fulfilled. (John 17:11-12)

> O righteous Father, although the world has not known You, yet I have known You; and these have known that You sent Me; and I have made Your name known to them, and will make it known, so that the love with which You loved Me may be in them, and I in them. (John 17:25-26)

After Jesus said, "I and the Father are one" in John 10:30, the Jews threatened to stone Him. From the verses we just read in John 17, it is easy to see Jesus' declaration includes being one with the Father in name also.

Isaiah predicted the birth of Christ centuries before the event. Notice carefully what the name of this son would be:

> For a child will be born to us, a son will be given to us; And the government will rest on His shoulders; And His name will be called Wonderful Counselor, Mighty God, Eternal Father, Prince of Peace. (Isaiah 9:6)

Among other things, the name of this son would be the *Mighty God* and the *Eternal Father*. While Jesus came to Earth to do many things, clearly He also came to reveal to us the saving name of His Father and our God! By examining Peter's apparent mistake, we learn an awesome truth about the name of the Father—that it is in fact the same as the name of the Son.

In Acts 2, did Peter baptize in the name of the Father when he baptized in the name of Jesus Christ? Since we have seen how Jesus rightly ascribed the Father's name to Himself, and this is what Peter said and did, then he obeyed this part of the commission as well. It was hard for me to grasp this the first time I examined it. You might be thinking the same thing, but it is undeniable when carefully examined from Scripture. We see in other New Testament passages that the apostle Paul also understood the Father's name to be Jesus. For example, he instructed believers to thank the Father by using the name of Jesus Christ: "Always giving thanks for all things in the name of our Lord Jesus Christ to God, even the Father." (Ephesians 5:20) "Whatever you do in word or deed, do all in the name of the Lord Jesus, giving thanks through Him to God the Father." (Colossians 3:17)

The name of the Holy Spirit

What about the name of the Holy Spirit? Can the name of the Holy Spirit possibly be Jesus too? Where can we find the answer? In John 14 Jesus explained that He is the One who will come to us as the Helper (KJV "Comforter"), which is the Holy Spirit, which Jesus said would be sent in His name:

> I will ask the Father, and He will give you another Helper, that He may be with you forever; *that is* the Spirit of truth, whom the world cannot receive, because it does not see Him or know Him, *but* you know Him because He abides with you and will be in you. I will not leave you as orphans; I will come to you. (John 14:16)

> But the Helper, the Holy Spirit, whom the Father will send in My name, He will teach you all things, and bring to your remembrance all that I said to you. (John 14:26)

If Jesus claimed to be the Helper/Comforter, which is the Holy Spirit, which the Father sent in the name of Jesus Christ, then we have this part of our answer as well—Jesus is indeed the name of the Holy Spirit. We see that Peter undeniably baptized in the name of the Holy Spirit when he invoked the name of Jesus Christ at this post-resurrection baptismal precedent.

Conclusion

What do we learn from this worthwhile examination? We can unmistakably conclude that Peter obeyed Jesus' command in Matthew 28:19 when he baptized in the name of Jesus Christ, which is the name of the Father, Son and Holy Spirit. This certainly helps us see why the name of Jesus Christ is above every other name!

Rather than repeating the words "Father, Son, and Holy Spirit," it appears conclusive that Peter understood and obeyed exactly what Jesus commanded him to do. From this example, we see a very powerful truth about the name of Jesus Christ. We also observe the intended application of calling on Jesus' name at baptism for salvation from sins. A thorough study will reveal this is not an isolated incident, but the standard practice of the New Testament church. Closely examining the examples where believers obey the good news will remove any doubt of the Bible's intended pattern of applying the gospel of Jesus Christ for us today.

Would Peter have obeyed Jesus' command had he not invoked the name of Jesus Christ at baptism? The answer appears to be no. If Peter disobeyed Christ's command when he used the actual name of the Son, Father and Holy Spirit (Jesus Christ), then all those at the church's foundation obeyed a misguided teaching and were not baptized according to Jesus' plan. Since Peter was given the keys to the kingdom of heaven by Christ, and based upon the scriptural evidence about the name, we can be certain he followed Christ's commands precisely.

What about the other apostles?

At this pivotal moment in Christian history, Peter stood up with the other apostles as he preached and gave the hearers instructions to repent and be baptized in the name of Jesus Christ for the forgiveness of sins. (See Acts 2:14) That the other apostles stood near Peter is important because they obviously did not object or correct him, but remained united. Because of this, we can conclude that they agreed with how Peter carried out the Great Commission and similarly understood this was what Jesus expected them to do.

Additional points

Considering what we have just seen, it makes sense to look again at the Bible's command to "do all in the name of the Lord Jesus, giving thanks through Him to God the Father." (Colossians 3:17)

This evidence further reinforces how we should follow Jesus' Commission; by actually invoking the name of Jesus rather than merely repeating His instructions to baptize as stated in Matthew 28:19. To fulfill His charge, we must do as Peter did—call on the name of Jesus Christ, for there is salvation in no other name. (See Acts 4:10-12)

Understanding this subject took a while to absorb as what it meant began to sink in, along with what I needed to do about it. Perhaps you are contemplating the same things. While you do, take a look at how other believers applied the gospel message by faith when they come to Christ.

Samaritan believers

Remember, we're looking for examples where people were actually obeying the gospel for the first time, not receiving post-conversion instructions or glimpsing important verses that simply address the need of salvation. The Samaritan conversion account is recorded in Acts 8, where Philip traveled to Samaria and preached the good news about the kingdom of God and the name of Jesus Christ. As we read carefully, we will see the same pattern followed as by the Jews in Acts 2:

> But when they believed Philip preaching the good news about the kingdom of God and the name of Jesus Christ, they were being baptized, men and women alike. Even Simon himself believed; and after being baptized, he continued on with Philip, and as he observed signs and great miracles taking place, he was constantly amazed. Now when the apostles in Jerusalem heard that Samaria had received the word of God, they sent them Peter and John, who came down and prayed for them that they might receive the Holy Spirit. For He had not yet fallen upon any of them; they had simply been baptized in the name of the Lord Jesus. Then they *began* laying their hands on them, and they were receiving the Holy Spirit. Now when Simon saw that the Spirit was bestowed through the laying on of the apostles' hands, he offered them money, saying, "Give this authority to me as well, so that everyone on whom I lay my hands may receive the Holy Spirit." (Acts 8:12-19)

Here is a synopsis of how they accepted the good news of salvation by faith:

1. They obeyed with the *death of Christ* by turning their faith away from Simon's sorceries and toward Jesus (an act of repentance)
2. They identified with the *burial of Christ* by being baptized in the name of Jesus Christ (buried with Him in baptism for the forgiveness of sins)
3. They obeyed the *resurrection of Christ* by receiving the Holy Spirit, which happened after placing their faith in Jesus and baptism

The Bible does not specifically say the Samaritans spoke with other languages when they received the Holy Spirit. However, we know there was obviously a God-given manifestation as this happened, for verse 18 records that Simon saw something extraordinary when the believers received the Holy Spirit. If the Samaritans had stood still and silently "accepted Jesus Christ," would Simon have been wild to purchase that sign? I'm personally convinced he saw (and doubtlessly heard) them speak with other languages, as this would be consistent with Acts 2, and the examples to come in Acts 10 and 19. This also agrees with Jesus' mini-parable in John 3:8 about the sound heard with all that are born of the Spirit. As we saw previously in Mark 16:17, Jesus said believers should expect this to happen.

Gentile believers obey the gospel

The Jews, then the Samaritans had faith in the gospel by applying it in exactly the same way. Now we move to Acts 10 to see if the first Gentile believers followed this pattern also. If you see there is more you can apply to your life through this account, don't be afraid to act upon it or ask for it. If we ask, we will receive. God is willing to give His Spirit to us, if we will simply ask Him.[1]

---

[1] See Luke 11:9-13.

Observe Cornelius, a God-believer who had an impressive spiritual résumé even before he accepted the Lordship of Christ through the gospel. While his good works and earnestness had not placed him in right standing with God, they did get God's attention. Because of Cornelius's love and sincerity, God sent Peter to preach the gospel to him, and to give him and his family an opportunity to obey the good news by faith. I believe there are many like Cornelius today, to whom God would like to impart this same wonderful measure of grace. We see his story in Acts 10:

> There was a certain man in Caesarea called Cornelius, a centurion of the band called the Italian *band, A* devout *man,* and one that feared God with all his house, which gave much alms to the people, and prayed to God alway[s]. He saw in a vision evidently about the ninth hour of the day an angel of God coming in to him, and saying unto him, Cornelius. And when he looked on him, he was afraid, and said, What is it, Lord? And he said unto him, Thy prayers and thine alms are come up for a memorial before God. And now send men to Joppa, and call for *one* Simon, whose surname is Peter: He lodgeth with one Simon a tanner, whose house is by the sea side: he shall tell thee what thou oughtest to do. (Acts 10:1-6 KJV)

Cornelius was a generous Italian centurion who prayed often and feared God. One day at about three in the afternoon, an angel appeared to him, telling him to send to Joppa for a man called Peter who would tell Cornelius what to do.

Therefore, Cornelius's sincerity, generosity, God-fearing and belief had not qualified him for Heaven—for they didn't clothe him with the righteousness of Jesus Christ. That could come only if he chose to apply the gospel through faith. This is why the angel said that Peter would tell Cornelius what he "ought to do."

On Peter's end, it took a divine vision to teach him that God was no respecter of persons; that the gospel was for Gentiles as well as Jews. Therefore, Peter left what he'd been doing in Joppa and followed Cornelius's messengers to Caesarea to speak to a Gentile household. Several Jewish Christians went with him.

When he got there, Peter didn't waste time, but immediately began to preach to the hungry Gentiles. He hardly got the words out of his mouth before God did something that shocked the Jewish believers. God poured out the gift of His Spirit on Gentiles. They knew this was true because they heard them speaking with tongues and exalting God: [2]

> While Peter was still speaking these words, the Holy Spirit fell upon all those who were listening to the message. All the circumcised believers who came with Peter were amazed, because the gift of the Holy Spirit had been poured out on the Gentiles also. For they were hearing them speaking with tongues and exalting God. Then Peter answered, (Acts 10:44-46)

Even after this marvelous infilling, these Gentiles had not fulfilled all the gospel commands. They had obeyed the death of Christ by turning to God in repentance, and they had obeyed the resurrection of Christ by receiving the Holy Spirit. However, they still had one thing left—to obey the burial of Christ at baptism in the name of the Father, Son, and Holy Spirit—Jesus Christ.

Peter, realizing that these Gentiles still hadn't completed their gospel-applying process, turned to the surprised Jews and challenged if any could refuse water baptism to these people who have just received the Holy Spirit. When no one answered, Peter immediately ordered the Gentiles to be baptized in the name of Jesus Christ:

> "Surely no one can refuse the water for these to be baptized who have received the Holy Spirit just as we *did,* can he?" And he ordered them to be baptized in the name of Jesus Christ. Then they asked him to stay on for a few days. (Acts 10:47-48)

In Acts 10, we again see why this specific water baptism is so essential, and why believers must obey all components of the good news when they place their faith in Jesus Christ. The gospel

---

[2] It is important to note that this is the only New Testament precedent of people receiving the Holy Spirit at the same time they believed the gospel of Jesus Christ.

contains the power of God to save us from our sins, and we see that calling on His name at baptism accesses God's forgiveness. This is so important because it is where His blood is applied, covering our sins as the water covers our bodies:

> Of Him all the prophets bear witness that through His name everyone who believes in Him receives forgiveness of sins. (Acts 10:43)

In conclusion, we can see that these Gentile believers accepted Christ by obeying the gospel in the same way as the Jews and Samaritans:

1. They accepted the gospel message of Jesus Christ from their heart (*repentance/death*)
2. They identified with the burial of Jesus Christ (*baptism/burial*)
3. They received the Holy Spirit (*Spirit infilling/resurrection*)

The pattern is clear

It is becoming undeniably clear that when the earliest believers responded to the gospel by faith, they consistently did so by accepting the message of Christ's death, burial, and resurrection. This involved repenting, being baptized in the name of Jesus Christ for the forgiveness of sins, and receiving the supernatural infilling of the Spirit of Christ, which was evidenced consistently by a sound—speaking with other languages, which was foretold by Christ.

So when and why did this practice of obeying the gospel cease from being a normal part of Christian practice? We will explore this subject soon. For now let's continue to the next example in Acts 19, where we find more sincere believers walking in all the truth they know. When they become aware that God has more for them, they are willingly *re-baptized* in the name of Jesus Christ and are filled with the Holy Spirit, which is consistent with the established gospel pattern we have studied so far. Seeing this provided yet another reason that I chose to obey this scriptural teaching by re-responding to the gospel:

It happened that while Apollos was at Corinth, Paul passed through the upper country and came to Ephesus, and found some disciples. He said to them, "Did you receive the Holy Spirit when you believed?" And they *said* to him, "No, we have not even heard whether there is a Holy Spirit." And he said, "Into what then were you baptized?" And they said, "Into John's baptism." Paul said, "John baptized with the baptism of repentance, telling the people to believe in Him who was coming after him, that is, in Jesus." When they heard this, they were baptized in the name of the Lord Jesus. And when Paul had laid his hands upon them, the Holy Spirit came on them, and they *began* speaking with tongues and prophesying. (Acts19:1-6)

When Paul arrived in Ephesus, he found several believing disciples, but they were still following John the Baptist's teaching. Paul piqued their interest when he asked them if they received the Holy Spirit when they believed, and how they were baptized. Paul saw an opportunity to shine more gospel light into these sincere lives. He said, "John baptized with the baptism of repentance, telling the people to believe on Him who was coming after Him, that is, in Jesus." When the disciples heard this, they immediately wanted Paul to baptize them in the name of the Lord Jesus. When Paul laid his hands on them, they were filled with the Holy Spirit, evidenced by the sound of speaking with other tongues.

We can glean some essential details from observing this important passage:

- These people already believed, but didn't yet have the Holy Spirit
- Paul checked their baptism and re-baptized them because he knew the connection of baptism in Jesus' name to the promise of receiving the Holy Spirit
- These honest, openhearted believers welcomed the chance to do (or redo) things to please God and be faithful to scriptural teaching
- God is consistent in the way he fills people with the Holy Spirit. We can absolutely expect the same experience as in these Bible examples, for the promise is to all (See Acts 2:39)
- As believers, we should expect to speak with new languages as a normal part of Christian life (See the promise of Jesus in Mark 16)

- You too can have this same infilling if you will ask, seek, and knock—and if you will simply be baptized (or re-baptized, as these believers were) in Jesus' name, God promises to give you the gift of His Spirit

Again, this fourth example illustrates believers' acceptance of the gospel message by obeying Jesus' death, burial and resurrection:

1. These believers had already turned to God in *repentance* and were living in all the truth they had received so far
2. Though already baptized, they were *re-baptized* in Jesus' name, because calling upon His name for salvation is so important and powerful, it was consistently done at all post-resurrection baptisms to obey the Great Commission commands of Jesus
3. They were *born of the Holy Spirit* once they obeyed the instructions of the apostle Paul. As they were filled, they spoke with other languages/tongues

The conversion of Saul

Saul of Tarsus is introduced as a great enemy of the church, but later becomes an even greater friend to it as the apostle Paul. On his way to Damascus to bind and imprison believers in Jesus, a blinding light shone from heaven, and God's declaration changed Saul's life. The Lord then told a disciple named Ananias to go pray for Saul. At first hesitant, Ananias finally went as directed, greeted his former enemy, laid hands on him and had him baptized:

So Ananias departed and entered the house, and after laying his hands on him said, "Brother Saul, the Lord Jesus, who appeared to you on the road by which you were coming, has sent me so that you may regain your sight and be filled with the Holy Spirit." And immediately there fell from his eyes something like scales, and he regained his sight, and he got up and was baptized; (Act 9:17-18)

In this passage, the Bible doesn't say how he was baptized, but Paul later recounted the episode in Acts 22:

'Now why do you delay? Get up and be baptized, and wash away your sins, calling on His name.' (Acts 22:16)

We often tell the story of Paul's Damascus Road experience, but there was more than the bright light and the voice from heaven. Paul went through the same gospel application that other believers had done. He turned (rather abruptly!) to Jesus in repentance and was baptized, calling on the name of the Lord, which is of course, Jesus Christ. We also know Paul was filled with the Holy Spirit and spoke in other languages because he wrote to the Corinthian believers, "I thank God, I speak in tongues more than you all" (1Corinthians 14:18)

Once again, the same pattern of obeying the gospel holds true:

1. Saul accepted the death of Christ by dying to sin at repentance
2. He partook in the burial of Christ at baptism, calling on the name of the Lord—Jesus Christ
3. He identified with the resurrection of Christ by receiving the same Holy Spirit that raised Christ from the tomb, evidenced by the supernatural evidence of speaking in an unlearned language

The Ethiopian eunuch

Let's take a look at some additional instances that reveal the same pattern of responding to the gospel. We'll save one for a later chapter, but here we'll look at the Ethiopian Eunuch in Acts 8 and Lydia of Philippi and her household in Acts 16.

God had told Philip to leave the great revival in Samaria and head south along the Gaza road. Not knowing what to expect, he came upon an Ethiopian, who was a man of authority serving under Queen Candace. Philip saw the man reading the writings of the prophet Isaiah and asked him if he understood the passage. The Ethiopian said he couldn't understand it without someone to explain it to him. He invited Philip to ride with him in his chariot. Philip then explained that the passage was about Jesus Christ and His crucifixion. From there, Philip explained the mission of Jesus, its culmination at Calvary, and the significance of all this for a person's salvation.

Philip obviously told him how to accept the same gospel plan of salvation he had preached in Samaria because, when the eunuch spotted a pool of water, he said, "Look! Water! What prevents me from being baptized?" Philip responded, "If you believe with all your heart, you may." The eunuch affirmed, "I believe that Jesus Christ is the Son of God." He ordered the chariot driver to stop, and both Philip and the eunuch went down into the pool and Philip baptized him. (See Acts 8:30-38)

Lydia

When Paul arrived in Philippi, he encountered a woman named Lydia who was a worshiper of God and a well-to-do fabric merchant. Paul preached to her, and the Lord "opened [Lydia's] heart to respond" to what Paul had told her. Her response was that she and all her household were baptized. (See Acts 16:14-15)

Admittedly, these two examples are slightly different from the previous ones in this respect—they don't record that these converts were filled with the Holy Spirit. However, the Bible doesn't say they *didn't* receive the Spirit—it just doesn't record it happening here. We know they were promised this infilling, because we have read that the promise of the gift of God's Spirit is for anyone who will turn to Him in repentance and be baptized in the name of Jesus Christ. It's safe to say we can know that God fulfilled His end of the bargain; we give Him our lives by faith in the gospel through repentance (death) and baptism (burial), and He gives us His forgiveness and Spirit (resurrection)—what a deal!

More evidence

This good news is available for all who will simply demonstrate faith to invite its grace and power. The following verses of Scripture confirm our access to the blood-applying, salvation-from-sin pattern of baptism in Jesus' name and the infilling of the Spirit:

> Such were some of you; but you were washed, but you were sanctified, but you were justified in the name of the Lord Jesus Christ and in the Spirit of our God. (1Corinthians 6:11)

What God does for believers through obedience to the gospel is not our works, but definitely His. Titus highlights this wonderful truth in chapter 3:

> He saved us, not on the basis of deeds which we have done in righteousness, but according to His mercy, by the washing of regeneration and renewing by the Holy Spirit, whom He poured out upon us richly through Jesus Christ our Savior, so that being justified by His grace we would be made heirs according to the hope of eternal life. (Titus 3:5-7)

The statement in verse 7 is a big one because it shows that our washing and infilling are agents of God's grace. Because of the blood of Jesus Christ and the gift of the Holy Spirit of God, we are saved by grace through faith. Paul wrote about this grace to the Ephesians who were saved by accepting the gospel in Acts 19:

> For by grace you have been saved through faith; and that not of yourselves, *it is* the gift of God; not as a result of works, so that no one may boast. For we are His workmanship, created in Christ Jesus for good works, which God prepared beforehand so that we would walk in them. (Ephesians 2:8-10)

I truly hope that no one reading this book believes for one second that it advocates a works-based salvation. That would be an erroneous position to hold or teach. Any saving thing that God imparts to us is a product of His grace. He won't force it on us; we merely permit Him to provide it through our faith. Without the blood of Christ shed at the cross of Calvary, no response on our part could ever save us. Demonstrating our faith in the death, burial and resurrection of Christ is merely how we allow God to convey His saving power.

What questions do these examples bring up?

As Scripture reveals this consistent blueprint for applying the good news, you might be contemplating some of the same things I did at the beginning of my search:

- Why wasn't I ever shown this in church?
- Where are the examples of the apostles leading their hearers through a sinner's prayer, or similar method of accepting Jesus Christ?

Try to find them as we might, there are no biblical examples of new believers merely repeating a sincere prayer to receive Christ. Instead, there are multiple examples of a very different pattern. This is a fair and honest observation that should understandably concern many sincere believers. The goal of pointing this out isn't to upset anyone, but merely to "contend earnestly for the faith which was once for all handed down to the saints." The Bible charges us to do this in the book of Jude, and it is a primary purpose of this book. If you are seeing this pattern for the first time, I hope you view it as a treasure and are rejoicing in your discovery. It also helps to remind ourselves that God continually desires to lead each of us into more truth as we purposely walk with Him by faith. Such leading is a priceless manifestation of His love.

If we want Heaven to be our home, we must of course "accept" Jesus Christ as our Lord and Savior. The examples of those who accepted His saving work in the Bible clearly reveal that obeying the gospel is the original and intended practice of doing so. If we proclaim His message of salvation, we must have faith to apply it just as Scripture reveals, because preparing people for eternity is the most important work on earth.

Stealing and restoring

Now that we have seen the consistent practice of obeying the gospel from Scripture, the questions bears asking: who would want to steal this wonderful practice away from the church? There is one, whom Jesus called a thief; that is, our enemy the devil. This subtle robber would also love to *keep* this practice away from us. Since the biblical pattern we are exploring might not have ever been in your denomination or recent background, he'd like to whisper in your ear; "You don't need to obey the gospel. You already believe. This really isn't a part of your heritage, anyway. You've made it this far, why rock the boat now?" Such subtleties speak to what we talked about in chapter 2; the further removed we are from any certain Bible practice, the harder it can be for the rightful heirs to accept and reinstate it, even when there's overwhelming proof it was the standard practice of our Christian family throughout the New Testament.

If the biblical plan of obeying the gospel was taken away from us, and if heaven must receive Christ until the times of restoration of all things (See Acts 3:21), we can know assuredly that God wants to restore this beautiful truth to us today. We have nothing to fear and everything to gain by allowing God to reinstate simple obedience to the good news, just as practiced in the Bible.

Personal testimony

I'll never forget when I saw and understood this for the first time. I was so excited to be re-baptized into the name of Jesus. I called my pastor on a Friday in March and insisted that he baptize me that night. It was cold and we were outside in a lake when I received remission of my sins—and I could not have been happier!

That night I experienced an undeniable difference as I was clothed with Christ by being buried with Him in baptism. There was no comparison to my previous ceremony where the minister said, "I baptize you in the name of the Father, and of the Son, and of the Holy Spirit." Even though I was much younger, I still remember being disappointed when there was no change. However, when I was baptized in the name of Jesus Christ, there was such undeniable power of His blood being applied to my life. I literally experienced the weight of my sin disappear as we called on the name of the Lord. If you haven't been baptized in the name of Jesus Christ, you must experience it for yourself. It is that awesome!

I need to emphasize an important point here: to be re-baptized is not saying that your heart was wrong at a previous baptism, or that you weren't sincere. It only means that you haven't applied it as Scripture demonstrates and you naturally want to follow what God has led you to in His word. If this describes you, then please respectfully ask to be re-baptized in Jesus' name as the God-followers in Acts 19 did. I have yet to meet anyone who was disappointed after calling on the name of Jesus Christ at his or her baptism.

It really is so simple to identify with the biblical pattern of obeying the gospel. Merely respond or re-respond by repenting and being baptized in the same manner as practiced in Scripture. It is how we receive Gods promises to save us from our sins and fill us with His Spirit, if we have yet to receive it.

Objections to speaking with other languages

This topic will be addressed in more detail later, but for now, I'd like to share my experiences.

To those who may not agree that receiving the Holy Spirit is initially evidenced by speaking with other languages today, I can only testify about what is in the Bible and what I've seen and heard myself. I have personally witnessed hundreds if not thousands of people from children to seniors speak with other languages as they receive the Spirit. My witness doesn't even touch the tremendous outpourings of the Holy Spirit in many crusades and churches around the world. This same Holy Spirit infilling is still happening today across geographical and denominational boundaries today because God promised to pour out His Spirit on all humanity, as recorded in the prophecies of Joel.

Jesus said a sound would be associated with *everyone* that is born of the Spirit, and that the sign of speaking with tongues would follow believers. (See John 3:8, Mark 16:17) It doesn't appear as if He placed a time constraint on this promise.

Many have received the Spirit with this same initial biblical evidence after previously believing they automatically had the Spirit when they believed. Because of their prior teaching, they never saw the need to *ask* God for it. When they did ask, they were filled just as those in the Bible were. In my early believing years, I never personally considered that I should ask to be filled with the Holy Spirit, but this is what Jesus told us to do, and what to thirst for and expect. (See Luke 9, John 7)

It's true that we receive things from God because we simply ask. If we desire something from the Lord, we are to ask, seek and knock. Does that describe the way we seek God? I didn't previously receive the Holy Spirit because I simply didn't ask for it. I had not because I asked not. When I asked, I received the Holy Spirit and spoke with an unlearned language just as the Bible converts did. Again, it was the greatest thing that had ever happened in my life. I'd like to challenge you to diligently seek God and ask Him to fill you as you've seen in the Bible. If He did it for me, He will do it for you.

Why so many illustrations?

Why does the Bible provide so many examples of conversions, and what does it mean for us today? God is making sure we can see exactly what it means to obey the gospel and not to accept any pattern that is outside of His. If there are places in the New Testament where people followed another plan as they applied the gospel, where are the accounts?

If we cannot establish a biblical precedent for other practices, we can be confident God wants us to simply follow His Word. We'll never regret acting in agreement with the scriptural method. The Bible doesn't say the early church stopped practicing the gospel-obedience message nor does it predict a time where it would be OK to abandon this instruction. On the contrary, it shows us where believers continued devoting themselves to this teaching:

> Peter said to them, "Repent, and each of you be baptized in the name of Jesus Christ for the forgiveness of your sins; and you will receive the gift of the Holy Spirit. For the promise is for you and your children and for all who are far off, as many as the Lord our God will call to Himself." And with many other words he solemnly testified and kept on exhorting them, saying, "Be saved from this perverse generation!" So then, those who had received his word were baptized; and that day there were added about three thousand souls. They were continually devoting themselves to the apostles' teaching and to fellowship, to the breaking of bread and to prayer. (Acts 2:38-42)

Indeed, this sound advice still applies to us today.

6

OLD TESTAMENT FORESHADOWING

We hinted earlier about Old Testament examples that foreshadowed obeying the gospel. As we examine some of these types, they will further validate God's intended plan of good news application for us today.

Moses' Tabernacle in the wilderness

In Exodus, we see the plan for Israel's approach to God and a beautiful type of God's New Testament pattern. The short version is that after God delivered Israel from Egyptian bondage, he instituted a tabernacle used as a place for worship, sacrifice, and atonement. This structure served to bring Israel into God's presence and right standing with Him. The tent-like edifice moved with them as they traveled and consisted of different materials and stations. These stations parallel the New Testament pattern of our acceptance of the gospel message by faith.

God instructed Moses to use acacia wood to build the first structure within the tabernacle, the bronze altar. (See Exodus 27) God described it, gave the dimensions, and said it should be overlaid with bronze. Here, the blood of animals was shed as they died sacrificially—a type of the death of Christ, and of our death to sin at repentance. The priests would then proceed to the next station to wash their hands and feet at the bronze laver of water:

> The LORD spoke to Moses, saying, "You shall also make a laver of bronze, with its base of bronze, for washing; and you shall put it between the tent of meeting and the altar, and you shall put water in it. "Aaron and his sons shall wash their hands and their feet from it; when they enter the tent of meeting, they shall wash with water, so that they will not die; or when they approach the altar to minister, by offering up in smoke a fire *sacrifice* to the LORD. "So they shall wash their hands and their feet, so that they will not die; and it shall be a perpetual

statute for them, for Aaron and his descendants throughout their generations." (Exodus 30:17-21)

Notice this washing was to be a statute to them forever, not only when Israel was under the Law. The New Testament fulfillment of this statute is to wash our sins away by Christ's blood at the waters of our baptism/burial with Christ. Just as the priests would die if they didn't wash, so will we if we aren't washed from our sins. (See James 1:15)

After the priests washed in the laver, it was time to enter the Holy Place. In it were three items of furniture: the table of bread, the golden lamp stand, and the altar of incense. There are differences of opinion about what these typified, and this description is not intended to be an exhaustive study on the tabernacle. It is my opinion these were types of the Word of God (table of bread), illumination of the Spirit of God (golden lamp stand), and prayer (altar of incense). Just as we need the Word, God's Spirit, and prayer to understand, be led by, and approach God, the high priest needed these before entering into the next part of the tabernacle, the Holy of Holies, or Holiest Place.

The Holiest Place was where the Ark of the Covenant was, along with the mercy seat—where the direct presence of God met with the high priest. Here the high priest sprinkled the sacrificial blood that atoned for the sins of the entire nation of Israel. This is an undeniable foreshadowing of being filled with the presence and power of the Holy Spirit. We even see the New Testament writer of Hebrews refer to this tabernacle as a symbol for the present time:

> Now even the first covenant had regulations of divine worship and the earthly sanctuary. For there was a tabernacle prepared, the outer one, in which were the lampstand and the table and the sacred bread; this is called the holy place. Behind the second veil there was a tabernacle which is called the Holy of Holies, having a golden altar of incense and the ark of the covenant covered on all sides with gold, in which was a golden jar holding the manna, and Aaron's rod which budded, and the tables of the covenant; and above it were the cherubim of glory overshadowing the mercy seat. . . . Now when these things have been so prepared, the priests are continually

entering the outer tabernacle performing the divine worship, but into the second, only the high priest enters once a year, not without taking blood, which he offers for himself and for the sins of the people committed in ignorance. The Holy Spirit is signifying this, that the way into the holy place has not yet been disclosed while the outer tabernacle is still standing, which is a symbol for the present time. Accordingly both gifts and sacrifices are offered which cannot make the worshiper perfect in conscience, (Hebrews 9:1-9)

If just leaving Egypt and following God were enough for the Hebrews, there would have been no need for the tabernacle. However, God didn't just want believers, He wanted those believers to be brought into a righteous standing with Him, which was the purpose of God's tabernacle plan.

Thankfully, God sent His Son, Christ Jesus, to be our high priest, who fulfilled this old plan:

But when Christ appeared as a high priest of the good things to come, He entered through the greater and more perfect tabernacle, not made with hands, that is to say, not of this creation; (Hebrews 9:11)

Paul explained that the New Testament temple (our body) is the equivalent of the Old Testament tabernacle when he wrote, "Do you not know that you are a temple of God and that the Spirit of God dwells in you? If any man destroys the temple of God, God will destroy him, for the temple of God is holy, and that is what you are." (1Corinthians 3:16-17) "Or what agreement has the temple of God with idols? For we are the temple of the living God..." (2Corinthians 6:16)

With this Old Testament example, we see the following:

· A necessity for a sacrificial death for sins
· A water washing that prepared the way to come into the place of God's dwelling
· The most Holy Place of God's presence for that era

This is a clear foreshadowing of the New Testament plan of faith in Christ through death to sin at repentance, water baptism/burial with Christ Jesus for the washing of sins, and the most Holy union of man and God possible on Earth in this age, the infilling of God's Holy Spirit.

The Garden of Eden

As far back as Genesis 3, we see a type of the gospel message that requires our cooperation to accept God's solution. After Adam and Eve sinned, God came to them with a plan that allowed an animal to die as a sacrificial substitute for their guilt, and garments of skin were provided to cover their exposed condition. (See Genesis 3:21)

In this scenario, Adam and Eve had a choice; they could simply believe that God provided a sacrifice for their nakedness (and remain uncovered), or they could demonstrate faith in the substitution by putting on the sacrificial garments to have their sin-exposed condition remedied. Look at what happened when they clothed themselves with what God provided. Not only were they covered, but then every time God looked at them afterwards:

- He saw His work of substitution covering them, instead of their own inadequate attempts
- He was reminded of His sacrificial provision for His creation
- He remembered how His judgment for their sin came upon the sacrifice instead of Adam and Eve

God's substitute in the Garden of Eden is a beautiful type of New Testament salvation, where we witness our Savior dying sacrificially to provide a covering for humanity's sins. While this act was for all, we must still "clothe ourselves" with the work of Jesus Christ by faithfully accepting His saving gospel. The Bible repeatedly demonstrates this is where we receive His freely given grace by faith, "For [you] are all sons of God through faith in Christ Jesus. For all of you who were baptized into Christ have clothed yourselves with Christ." (Galatians 3:26-27)

We can and should believe that Christ's sacrifice will render us innocent. However, if we only look at Calvary's cross with gratitude without clothing ourselves with Christ according to the biblical pattern, our sins will remain uncovered. The wonderful thing about baptism into Christ Jesus is that it allows God to observe His finished work of substitution on us and remember the blood He shed. He then sees His own innocence instead of our transgression, or our attempts at a religious cover-up. Like the insufficiency of the fig leaves in the garden, anything outside of applying the gospel is inadequate to cover our sins today.

David wrote, "How blessed is he whose transgression is forgiven, Whose sin is covered!" (Psalm 32:1)

Exiting Egypt

First Corinthians recalls the Hebrews exodus from Egypt. It specifically describes what happened after they left their lives as slaves by faith as "baptisms." They passed through the waters of the Red Sea and were sheltered by a pillar of cloud. This was a foreshadowing of our New Testament water and Spirit baptisms, which are the next two elements of obeying the gospel after we turn our backs on our slavery to sin at repentance:

> For I do not want you to be unaware, brethren, that our fathers were all under the cloud and all passed through the sea; and all were baptized into Moses in the cloud and in the sea; and all ate the same spiritual food; and all drank the same spiritual drink, for they were drinking from a spiritual rock which followed them; and the rock was Christ.. (1Corinthians 10:1-4)

Just as the people of God partook of the same experiences on their saving journey from the bondage of Egypt, we must be willing to leave our old lifestyle of sin and enjoy the saving benefits of water and Spirit baptisms today. Why would a believer settle for anything less?

7

CALLING ON THE NAME OF THE LORD FOR SALVATION

How will they call on Him?

It is a widely accepted Christian truth that a believer must confess Jesus Christ with their mouth and believe in their heart that God raised Christ from the dead to be saved. We find this teaching in Romans 10, where Paul quoted from Joel 2. This highly significant passage instructs us to call on the name of Jesus Christ for salvation. It is worthwhile to note that Paul was addressing the universality of salvation for all people here, which was a big issue for many in his day.

Verse 16, as we have seen, provides a glimpse into just how hearers are to apply the message and exactly when they are to call on the Lord's name. Here is the important portion of scripture that immediately precedes this reference:

> But what does it say? "THE WORD IS NEAR YOU, IN YOUR MOUTH AND IN YOUR HEART"—that is, the word of faith which we are preaching, that if you confess with your mouth Jesus *as* Lord, and believe in your heart that God raised Him from the dead, you will be saved; for with the heart a person believes, resulting in righteousness, and with the mouth he confesses, resulting in salvation. For the Scripture says, "WHOEVER BELIEVES IN HIM WILL NOT BE DISAPPOINTED." For there is no distinction between Jew and Greek; for the same *Lord* is Lord of all, abounding in riches for all who call on Him; for "WHOEVER WILL CALL ON THE NAME OF THE LORD WILL BE SAVED." How then will they call on Him in whom they have not believed? How will they believe in Him whom they have not heard? And how will they hear without a preacher? How will they preach unless they are sent? Just as it is written, "HOW BEAUTIFUL ARE THE FEET OF THOSE WHO BRING GOOD NEWS OF GOOD THINGS!" (Romans 10:8-15)

Here is the prophecy quoted from Joel:

> It will come about after this that I will pour out My Spirit on all
> mankind; and your sons and daughters will prophesy, your old
> men will dream dreams, your young men will see visions. Even
> on the male and female servants I will pour out My Spirit in
> those days. . . . And it will come about that whoever calls on
> the name of the LORD will be delivered; … (Joel 2:28-32)

It is interesting that as Peter preached on the Day of Pentecost in
Acts 2, he referenced the same verse of Scripture just before he
directed his hearers to be baptized, calling on the name of the
Lord.

> 'AND IT SHALL BE THAT EVERYONE WHO CALLS ON THE
> NAME OF THE LORD WILL BE SAVED.' (Acts 2:21)

Honest observations about the Sinner's Prayer

There is a crucial point in Romans 10 that provoked my careful
consideration and prompted much of the study that went into my
decision to obey the gospel and to undertake the writing of this
book. We touched on this observation in chapter 1, and we will
address it more completely here. This important matter goes to the
heart of how believers respond to the good news: *while Romans
10 tells us what to do to be saved, it does not record anyone
actually doing it.* This might seem simplistic, but it is important to
understand that while these instructions were indeed carried out, it
didn't actually happen in Romans 10. We have to search for the
conversion examples as we did in chapter 5 to understand how
this actually took place.

When witnessing or preaching to the lost, we must lead them to
Jesus Christ according to biblical instruction and examples. While
it is popular to use Romans 10 as a springboard for applying New
Testament salvation, it is not only reasonable, but our obligation to
reveal where others in the Bible actually applied the principles
found in the passage.

Based on the volume of scriptural examples where people were actually accepting Christ, we do not find the apostles asking their hearers to repeat a sinner's prayer to accept Christ as their Savior—ever. I know this might be a sobering observation for many reading this book, but please continue. The closest example is the Philippian jailer in Acts 16, who was about to commit suicide because he thought all the prisoners in his charge had escaped. Paul told the frantic man to believe on the Lord and he would be saved. Then after he and everyone in his house had heard the word of the Lord, they decided to obey the gospel by being baptized to clothe themselves with Christ's saving righteousness. Because they first believed, they responded to the gospel by faith, and were saved.[1]

While many may look to the first part of the jailer's story as a method of salvation, we see that this family obeyed the gospel, consistent with all other New Testament conversion accounts. As we have seen, this is how believers were always instructed to demonstrate their believing faith and access the power of Christ's death, burial, and resurrection.

Paul didn't tell this seeking family to sincerely pray to receive Christ. If Paul would have said this as he preached to them, that's what they would have done. There's absolutely nothing wrong with a heartfelt prayer of repentance that asks God to come into one's life, but that alone is not what covers sins. As uncomfortable as it might sound, if merely saying a prayer of acceptance is God's plan for receiving salvation, why aren't there any examples of this actually happening in Scripture? Instead, we consistently find those who believed accepted the good news by faith through applying each saving part: repentance/death, baptism/burial, and the infilling of the Holy Spirit/resurrection.

---

[1] Like the examples of Lydia and the Ethiopian eunuch, it does not say here that the warden received the Holy Spirit—but neither does it say he didn't. We do know that upon being baptized in Christ's name the promise of receiving the Spirit was his.

What is God revealing?

An honest conclusion to this examination is that God is attempting to communicate a vital truth to us through the answers to these questions. The apostles always had their converts accept Christ through obeying the gospel by faith—and never by a sinner's prayer. The death, burial, and resurrection of Christ are truly the power of God unto salvation for those who will simply respond by agreeing with His saving work. Just as Christ had to experience a personal death, burial, and resurrection before leaving for Heaven, so must we.

Connecting the dots

Although no one is being converted in Romans 10, we see that verse 16 somehow connects obeying the gospel to calling on the name of the Lord for our salvation.

How does the Bible reconcile what might seem to be different teachings? The answer is simply this; while Romans 10 gives us the "what" to do, the "how" is plainly given to us by all of the examples of obeying the gospel message we have seen.

It doesn't take great powers of observation to notice that the biblical conversion examples differ greatly from the widespread current tradition of saying or repeating a prayer of acceptance. Although it was not easy to admit, I could not deny what I read and saw. I had to make the decision to place my trust in what I read above church custom and follow the biblical pattern, and I've never regretted it.

How then do we call on the name of Jesus Christ to be saved from our sins? Acts 22, along with the other examples we have seen, gives us the consistent answer. We must confess the name of Jesus Christ by calling upon that name as we are baptized, for this is where our sins are washed away by the application of His blood by faith:

'Now why do you delay? Get up and be baptized, and wash away your sins, calling on His name.' (Acts 22:16)

Many might still construe this verse as a declaration that water saves us from our sins. Again, that is not what I believe, for only the blood of Jesus Christ can wash away our sins. There is no substitute.

We know from 1John 5 that the Spirit, water, and blood agree. This is never truer than at our burial with Christ. While some may not have considered that calling on His name at baptism is where we allow His blood to be applied to our lives, it is undoubtedly the consistent New Testament pattern. When a convert is being baptized, the saving name of Jesus Christ must be invoked, for this is where the water, blood and the promise of the Spirit agree for believers.

According to Scripture, we must call on the name of the Lord to be saved. Acts 22:16 provides a tremendous insight into how applying the blood and calling on the name of Jesus Christ for salvation are biblically connected at baptism.

Applying the Passover blood

At the historic Passover event that preceded the Exodus, a lamb was slaughtered to provide a protective blood covering for each family that wanted to escape the coming destroyer. Notice what God required of those who believed in His command: not only did the believing Hebrews have to have faith that the blood would be sufficient to protect them, they had to *do* something with the blood to receive it's protection.

They were commanded to take a basin of the slain lamb's blood, dip a hyssop branch into it, and apply the blood to the doorposts and lintel of the house where they had eaten the Passover lamb. They were then to remain inside the safety of the home. That night the Lord would pass through the land and the destroyer would kill all the firstborn, but when the Lord caught sight of the lamb's blood, He would not allow the destroyer to slay anyone in that house. (See Exodus 12:7-23)

This story typifies an important principle that is vital to us today. While the blood was in the basin, it was certainly sufficient to protect those in the house, but not until it was applied by faith. Applying the blood was how they accessed God's promise of protection.

Would the Hebrews have been saved from the destroyer if they failed to apply the blood? Unfortunately, they would not have. They could have believed the blood was capable of protecting them as much as they liked, but without following the command to apply it, they would have forfeited God's intended protection.

Today, we believe the blood of Jesus Christ has the power to deliver us from the destructive consequences of sin. However, just as the Hebrews had to demonstrate faith by applying the sacrificial blood of their slain lamb for protection, we must also demonstrate faith as directed in Scripture to apply the blood of Christ, the slain Lamb of God, to protect our lives from sin.

This is why responding to the gospel as the Bible instructs is so effective. It is where we accept and apply the blood of Jesus Christ. Jesus made this application so easy in Mark 16 when He said to believe the gospel and be baptized for salvation. This is why all of the conversion examples show this consistent response to the gospel. Just as God's children in Egypt applied the blood to their homes by faith, we also apply the blood of Christ to our lives through our faith-response to the gospel message at baptism, calling on His name to be saved. This is how we demonstrate saving faith in the blood of Jesus Christ—accessing salvation through His name.

Are you putting Me on?

We have seen Galatians 3 point out that we can become children of God by faith, because those who are baptized into Christ "clothe themselves with Christ." As we saw in every conversion example, we must call on the name of the Lord at baptism, even if it means being re-baptized to obey the command.[2] Yes, we need faith in Christ for salvation, and being baptized with Christ is exactly *how* that faith is revealed. Other passages also support this vital teaching:

> Is it not they who slander and blaspheme that precious name by which you are distinguished and called [the name of Christ invoked in baptism]? (James 2:7 AMP)

> That the residue of men might seek after the Lord, and all the Gentiles, upon whom my name is called, saith the Lord, who doeth all these things. (Acts 15:17 KJV)

> Whatever you do in word or deed, *do* all in the name of the Lord Jesus, giving thanks through Him to God the Father. (Colossians 3:17)

> and that repentance for forgiveness of sins would be proclaimed in His name to all the nations, beginning from Jerusalem. (Luke 24:47)

> Of Him all the prophets bear witness that through His name everyone who believes in Him receives forgiveness of sins. (Acts 10:43)

The Bible records no other example of where the apostles had people to call on the name of Jesus Christ for salvation from their sins outside of baptism. Nor is there ever an example of anyone being baptized by invoking the titles, "Father, Son, and Holy Spirit." Although these titles refer to God, they are not His name.

If there is no other name besides Jesus that can save us, we must ask ourselves why *wouldn't* we want to call on the name of Jesus Christ at baptism, even if we only need to be re-baptized to agree with Scripture? What would stop us? The act itself is so simple. The hard thing might be to change our traditions. When Peter told us to grow in grace and in the knowledge of God, we can't assume it will always be easy or comfortable. Growth rarely is.

---

[2] Acts 19:1-6

However, accepting any growth process revealed by Scripture is always worthwhile.

Calling on the name of the Lord... and not being saved

Jesus gave an example of some people who called on His name, but were not allowed to enter the kingdom of Heaven. He concluded that only "he who does the will of My Father who is in heaven will enter the kingdom of heaven." (Matthew 7:21) When the people clamored that they had used His name for many things: prophesying, casting out demons and performing miracles, Jesus countered, "I never knew you; depart from me, you who practice lawlessness." (Matthew 7:23)

These believers plainly called on (and even ministered in) the name of the Lord and were rejected by God. Notice that Jesus says He *never* knew them. It wasn't that He used to, or once did. He never did. They called on the name of the Lord, and were lost.

Why wasn't their calling on His name sufficient? According to this example, there is obviously a way we can call on (and act in) the name of Christ that does not bring salvation. Where have we seen that calling on the name of Jesus saves us from our sins? If we believe the biblical examples, it is clearly when we are baptized, calling on the name of Jesus Christ. With this in mind, it becomes easy to understand why Paul was saddened in Romans 10 when people did not obey the gospel.

Another obvious example where calling on the name of the Lord doesn't save requires little explanation. Since the days of Moses, one of the Ten Commandments has been not to take the Lord's name in vain:

> "You shall not take the name of the LORD your God in vain, for the LORD will not leave him unpunished who takes His name in vain. (Exodus 20:7)

Calling Jesus Lord by the Holy Spirit

First Corinthians teaches us that we can call Jesus Lord only by the Holy Spirit. This points to two things: that only the Holy Spirit can connect our identity to Christ's resurrection, and it matters to God just *how* we call Him Lord:

> ...no one can say, "Jesus is Lord," except by the Holy Spirit (1Corinthians 12:3)

You might think this is a stretch, but when we say Jesus is Lord, we are really saying He is the One who is in control. We are saying that He has the right to direct us when we like it and even when our flesh doesn't like it. If He is Lord of our lives, we must give Him authority over our whole being, not just some portions of it. So how do we call Him Lord "by the Holy Spirit"? While there might be differences of opinion, we have seen those obeying Christ's resurrection allow God to control their speech as they were born of the Spirit. This is one way we allow Christ to have Lordship over the most difficult part of our bodies to control; our tongue—for James 3:8 states that "...no one can tame the tongue; *it is* a restless evil *and* full of deadly poison. "

Responding by faith to the king's invitation . . . and being lost

In Matthew 22:8-13, we see another man rejected by God, and at first, it doesn't seem fair. A king ordered a feast prepared and invitations sent out, possibly to the elite of the nation. But those invited in the first wave discounted the king's generosity and found excuses why they couldn't attend. The king then ordered that his servants go out into the streets and along the highways to invite anyone they met. Those in the second wave jumped at the chance to dine at the palace, and the banquet hall was filled with both good and evil guests. The king looked benevolently over the crowd until he spotted a man that stood out like a sore thumb. He approached him and asked, "How did you get in without a proper wedding garment?" When the man had nothing to say, the king ordered him bound and cast into outer darkness.

The man who responded eagerly to the king's invitation was thrown out of his presence into unimaginable horrors. The following are some of the ironic and tragic things about his situation:

- He was interested in the king's invitation
- He wanted to be a part of the marriage event
- He gratefully responded to the wedding invitation in faith
- He anticipated acceptance
- He was not adequately prepared by the one who invited him
- He had no explanation or understanding that he needed to "put on" appropriate wedding clothes to be acceptable to the king
- The king didn't notice if he was one of the good or bad guests; He was looking for something else
- The man had done everything he'd been instructed to do, yet he was horribly lost

The parallels to obeying the gospel in this passage are unmistakable. How many interested responders will be cast out when the king comes to see His guests on Judgment Day? What kind of "clothes" will the king be looking for? He'll be looking to see His righteousness upon us, the wedding garment. This will be the only clothing that will satisfy the king. When we have on His righteousness, God no longer sees our past sin, only His covering of innocence.

How do we put on the wedding garment of His righteousness? We have seen that we clothe ourselves with Christ by being buried with Him at baptism, calling on the name of Jesus Christ to be saved from our sins. This was so important that we saw the apostle Paul re-baptize an entire group of believers, simply because they had not been washed by this saving name. If Paul were able to visit our churches today, would he do anything different to prepare us for the arrival of the king?

Possible repercussions

It is fair to say that those close to us might not understand why we choose to demonstrate faith by applying newly received truths. They may even oppose our actions. Even if others don't agree, it would be nice if they would respect our motives for such important steps. Unfortunately, this may not always be the case. Jesus predicted this solemn reality in Matthew 10:34-38 when he declared that instead of coming to bring peace, He brought a sword. By this, He meant that family members would be at odds with each other: fathers/sons, mothers/daughters. He went so far as to say that a man's enemies would be members of his own household. Even if this is the case, we must continue to take up our cross and follow Him.

I remember how sobering it was when I discovered the marked contrast between how I was taught to respond to the gospel and how believers in the Bible did. I had to make a serious decision; whether to let the Bible guide me, or to disregard it and continue following a message that did not agree with the faith originally delivered to the church. What an extraordinary difference it made when I simply re-responded to be in agreement with the examples given in Scripture! The change was like night and day. I went from a traditional belief that Jesus died and rose again to experiencing for myself the power of the resurrection Spirit and remission of my sins.

"Lonely" faith

Deciding to re-respond by faith to the gospel was the best decision I ever made. I already had faith in God, but once I saw I had not applied the gospel as the Bible mandated, I wanted very much to please the Lord by obeying the good news. I could have let fear of my denomination's opinions or my family's religious traditions stop me, but I decided to exercise faith by following the instructions of God's Word. You may very likely have the same choice to make as you see what Scripture teaches. Even if it costs you something, you won't regret acting in agreement with the

Bible. Place your faith in the Word of God and seek its approval, direction, and teachings above anything else. Contend for the faith by demonstrating your faith through action. Indeed, faith demands that we act upon it, for James wrote:

> Therefore, putting aside all filthiness and all that remains of wickedness, in humility receive the word implanted, which is able to save your souls. But prove yourselves doers of the word, and not merely hearers who delude themselves. (James 1:21-22)

> Even so faith, if it hath not works, is dead, being alone. Yea, a man may say, Thou hast faith, and I have works: shew me thy faith without thy works, and I will shew thee my faith by my works. Thou believest that there is one God; thou doest well: the devils also believe, and tremble. But wilt thou know, O vain man, that faith without works is dead? (James 2:17-20 KJV)

Many contend that believers are saved by faith alone, which perhaps implies that responding in any way beyond heart trust somehow advocates salvation by works. We are certainly saved by faith in God, but responding to the gospel through obedience is how all post-resurrection believers allowed God to save them by faith. It is also interesting to note that the only place in the Bible where "faith" and "alone" are mentioned together is in the above passage that says faith without works is dead, or useless.

Too bold?

Suggesting that a believer re-respond to the gospel might sound bold, but I would pose these questions: Is boldly asking someone to obey the gospel a bad thing? If the devil can boldly tempt us to sin, and if the world demands that we conform to its actions and way of thinking, then how could someone asking a believer to obey the greatest message in history be a bad thing? In fact, anyone who would suggest that we obey the gospel of Jesus Christ is really acting in our eternal best interest.

If believers are ever going to stand upon the Word of God, today is the day. In light of a last-days spiritual climate where many won't endure sound teaching,[3] how can we close our eyes to what becomes so obvious upon studying the Scriptures? We will not have to answer to our church boards, friends, congregations, organizations, or families on the Day of Judgment, nor will they reward us. We must give account before God alone of the way we respond to the gospel.

If you decide to re-respond to the gospel, you will not be alone in this simple and wonderful step of faith. Dear believers all over the world know and understand this message, and would welcome the opportunity to share in this newfound part of your relationship with God. If someone has given a copy of this book to you, they may have already discovered how joyous it is to experience and walk in the truths you have seen from the Bible in these pages. Be encouraged to share your interest in obeying the gospel with them.

I believe you are going to have the greatest experience of your life by acting on the original pattern of applying the best possible news. Let me say in faith, you'll be so glad you did.

Conclusions

As certainly as God has fathered humanity, sent His Son to die as payment for our sins, and given His Holy Spirit to indwell and lead us, we can see a marvelous and very simple truth in how we must call on the name of the Lord. If we are ever going to invoke His name, we must do so when we are baptized. If we care about being true to the biblical pattern, we must use the name of the Father, Son, and Holy Spirit, which is Jesus Christ. The apostles understood this, for they had received the commission directly from Jesus Himself. They were the closest to Him and received His personal instruction. This was first-century teaching, not a baptismal practice arrived at much later in history, as we will document in the next chapter. No, the apostles never baptized

---

[3] See 2Timothy 4:3.

anyone by invoking the titles of Father, Son, and Holy Spirit. Instead, they called on the name of Jesus Christ in every instance.

In Colossians 3:17, Paul said we should do all in the name of the Lord Jesus. This includes baptism, the most important instance where we should call on His saving name. How will we call on Him? If we will simply emulate how New Testament believers called on Him, it will save us from our sins also. In light of the mountain of biblical evidence we have seen, we should be excited to be baptized or re-baptized, calling on the name of Jesus Christ.

When God reveals more of His Word to those who love Him, it in turn demonstrates His love for us. We continue to receive His love by applying the Word He brings to our awareness. Though it might sound uncomfortable, if we choose not to follow His Word, we are really choosing not to follow Him.

There is a reason why we do not find anyone in scripture coming to Christ by only repeating a prayer of acceptance. Praying a sincere prayer of repentance, asking God to come into our lives is an important thing—but it has no biblical precedent without also obeying the gospel.

To respond again to the gospel by faith is a simple thing. It may not be very comfortable to realize we have not fully obeyed this message, but our comfort must take a back seat to its complete application. If you are a believer that has seen the application of the gospel in a new light, please remember that re-responding to good news is a good idea, not a bad one. You will not regret it.

8

WHEN OBEYING THE GOSPEL CHANGED

With careful study followed by simple comparison, it becomes clear that some church practices are not in agreement with the scriptural precedents we have been examining. Therefore, the understandable question is; when did church leaders stop proclaiming the message of obeying the gospel as practiced in Scripture? We may not ever know all of the answers, but many are well documented, as we will see. The fact that this foundational practice is not followed in many churches is proof that Satan wanted to steal this from us, and has succeeded. He would certainly like it to remain missing—and consequently dead to us today.

The question of how this happened troubled me greatly as I saw how thorough the Bible is regarding the practice of applying the gospel, versus how differently my denomination had instructed me. It was obvious that something happened between the Bible examples and today. I suppose this was partly why Jude said to watch out for the undermining of the faith once given to the saints.[1]

Paul considered this a vital issue, too. In his letter to the church at Galatia, he noted that he couldn't believe how quickly they had deserted the gospel that was at first preached to them. They now believed a "different gospel," which was a misnomer because there really wasn't any other saving gospel. He stated, "...if any man is preaching to you a gospel contrary to what you received, he is to be accursed!" (See Galatians1:6-9)

Did the gospel Paul preached include the crucified and risen Jesus Christ? Absolutely. Did he preach that people must demonstrate their faith in the gospel by being baptized in the

---

[1] See Jude 3-4.

name of Jesus Christ, the one crucified for them? Yes, he did. Did he make sure they were born of the Spirit through receiving the Holy Spirit? Again, the answer is yes. Scripture is very explicit about us remaining faithful to this same preaching, and not allowing any substitute to take its place.

Documenting the changes to obeying the gospel

Respected historical sources verify that the early Christian church did not use a threefold baptismal formula but invoked the name of Jesus in baptism well into the second and third centuries. Here are some of the most common references available to substantiate this historical fact and address the change in the original, biblical pattern. Check them out for yourself:

Britannica Encyclopedia, 11th edit. vol. 3, 365-368:

Page 365: ". . . those who have been baptized into the name of the Lord—the normal formula of the New Testament."
Page 365: "In the third century baptism in the name of Christ was still so widespread that Pope Stephen, in opposition to Cyprian of Carthage, declared it to be valid."
Page 366: "Pope Nicholas, however (858-867) in the Responsa ad consulta Bulgarorum, allowed baptism to be valid tantum in nomine Christe, as in the Acts."
Page 366: "The formula of Rome is, 'I baptize thee in the name of Father and Son and Holy Spirit.'"
Page 368: "The apostolic age supplied this identification, and the normal use during it seems to have been 'into Christ Jesus', or 'in the name of the Lord Jesus Christ', or "of Jesus Christ' simply, or 'of the Lord Jesus Christ.' Paul explains these formulas as being equivalent to 'into the death of Christ Jesus', as if the faithful were in the rite raised from death to everlasting life. The likeness of the baptismal ceremony with Christ's death and resurrection ensured a real union with him of the believer who underwent the ceremony, according to the well known principle in sacris simulata pro veris accipi. . . . But as a rule the repentant underwent baptism in the

name of Jesus Christ, and washed away their sins before hands were laid on them unto reception of the Spirit."

Canney Encyclopedia of Religion, page 53:

"Persons were baptized at first 'in the name of the Lord Jesus' (Acts viii. 16, xix. 5). Afterwards, with the development of the doctrine of the Trinity, they were baptized 'in the name of the Father and of the Son and of the Holy Ghost' (cp. Justin Martyr, Apol. i. 61)."

Catholic Encyclopedia, (1913) vol. 2, page 263:

"The most probable opinion, however, seems to be that the terms 'in the name of Jesus', 'in the name of Christ', either refer to baptism in the faith taught by Christ, or are employed to distinguish Christian baptism from that of John the Precursor. It seems altogether unlikely that immediately after Christ had promulgated the trinitarian formula of baptism, the Apostles themselves would have substituted another. In fact, the words of St. Paul (Acts, xix) imply quite plainly that they did not."
"In the works of St. Ambrose . . . 'If you say Christ, you have designated God the Father, by whom the Son was anointed, and Him who anointed the Son, and the Holy Ghost in whom He was anointed.'"

New Catholic Encyclopedia, (1967) vol. 2, page 59:

". . . although Matthew (28.19) speaks of the Trinitarian formula, which is now used, the Acts of the Apostles (2.38; 8.16; 10.48; 19.5) and Paul (I Cor 1.13; 6.11; Gal 3.27, Rom 6.3) speak only of Baptism 'in the name of Jesus.' It has been proposed that the one being baptized had to confess the name of Jesus and then that the minister pronounced a Trinitarian formula (Crehan 76, 81)."
"While it is more obvious in the Matthaean formula (Mt. 28.19) that Baptism establishes a relationship to the triune God, it is no less

true when Baptism is given 'in the name of Jesus.' Since Baptism is an incorporation into Christ, it bestows at the same time the Holy Spirit (Acts 2.38; Eph 1.13; Gal 3.14; 4.6) and makes men children of the Father (Gal 4.6). It is conceivable that 'in the name of Jesus' meant nothing more than the candidate was given over to Christ, consecrated to Him, and submerged in Him (in His death)."

"After all, the validity of Baptism 'in the name of Jesus' was still accepted in the age of scholasticism."

"An explicit reference to the Trinitarian formula of Baptism cannot be found in the first centuries."

Hastings Encyclopedia of Religion, vol. 2, page 376-389:

Page 376: ". . . Peter appealed to for the terms of participation in the manifest Divine presence, should reply: 'Repent, and let each of you get baptized in the name of Jesus Messiah unto remission of your sins, and ye shall receive the free gift of the Holy Spirit,' and so escape the fate of 'this crooked generation'—revealed as such in its treatment of Messiah. This thought connected itself with the closing words of the passage just cited from Joel: 'And it shall be, that whosoever shall invoke the name of the Lord shall be saved,' i.e. from wrath in 'the day of the Lord, the great and notable day.' There was a recognized connection between solemn invocation of the Lord as Protector and the rite of baptism."

". . . confession of Jesus as Messiah or Lord (as Jahweh was Israel's Lord) and loyalty to the new and true allegiance (cf. Ac 20:21) appears from Ro 10:8ff, in allusion to the act of baptism. In that passage Christians are described as 'those who invoke Jesus as Lord,' J[oe]l 2:32 being cited in support of the description (cf Ac 9:14,21). 'With the mouth confession is made unto salvation' (Ro 10:10); that is the outward or objective side of the faith in the heart on which 'righteousness' is bestowed, and which expresses itself both in the water of baptism and in the word of the mouth to which Paul here directs attention."

"After 'baptism in the name of the Lord,' a man was regarded as 'in Christ' . . ."

Page 377-378: "'The Lord Jesus' seems, indeed, to grow out of the central phrase of the baptismal confession, viz., 'Jesus is Lord.'"
Page 378: "The use of a Trinitarian formula of any sort is not similarly suggested . . ."
Page 389: "The earliest form, represented in the Acts, was simple immersion . . . in water, the use of the name of the Lord, and the laying on of hands. To these were added, at various times and places which cannot be safely identified, (a) the trine name (Justin [Martyr]) . . . but the existing baptismal services strictly belong to the 3rd century."
"The earliest known formula is 'in the name of the Lord Jesus,' or some similar phrase; this is found in the Acts . . . but by the time of Justin Martyr the triune formula had become general."

Interpreter's Dictionary of the Bible, (1962), Pg. 349-351:

Page 349-350: ". . . baptism is spoken of specifically as 'in the name of Jesus Christ' (Acts 2:38; 10:48), or 'in the name of the Lord Jesus' (8:16; 19:5). Ordinarily baptism preceded the reception of the Holy Spirit, but in one instance—that of Cornelius—the gift of the Spirit was received before baptism; it is noteworthy that here, according to one account, Cornelius was subsequently baptized (10:48).
Page 351: "The evidence of Acts 2:38; 10:48 (cf. 8:16; 19:5), supported by Gal. 3:27; Rom. 6:3, suggests that baptism in early Christianity was administered, not in the threefold name, but 'in the name of Jesus Christ' or 'in the name of the Lord Jesus.'"

Hastings Dictionary of the Bible, (1963), page 88:

". . . baptism, to be done 'in the name of the Father and of the Son and of the Holy Spirit.' It thus takes up an early Christian liturgical formula which was not used before the second half of the first century. It is hardly possible to harmonize the universal aspect with the historical Jesus, and it is impossible to assume the trinitarian formula for the teaching in his lifetime."

"Different from the post-apostolic and later Christian liturgical praxis, which is marked by the trinitarian formula of Mt 28:19 (see Did. VII. i. 3 ; Just. Apol. LXI. 3, 11, 13) the primitive Church baptized 'in' or 'into' the name of Jesus. . . . The calling of a name effected—according to primitive belief—the presence of the divine person (or demon). Thus the spoken formula, 'in the name of Jesus,' effected the presence of the risen Lord and gave the baptized into His possession and protection. In this context the verb 'to seal' or the noun 'the seal' is often used (2 Co 1:22; perhaps also Ro 4:11; cf Eph 1:13 and Rev 7:3ff). In all these passages, which obviously set forth the earliest traditions, the [connection] of baptism with Christ's person and work is inherent. On the ground of this practice Paul can say; 'For as many of you as were baptized into Christ have put on Christ' (Gal 3:27). Referring in these words to 'rebirth' with Christ's resurrection, Paul presupposes that 'all of us who have been baptized into Christ Jesus were baptized into his death' (Ro 6:3). Thus baptism is no longer, as with John, only a cleansing from sins committed in the past, but is the act which sanctifies the present life and guarantees eschatological bliss. . . . The various elements may be summarized as follows: (a) The remission of sins . . . (b)The calling of the name of the Lord is an element concurrent with immersion. . . . (c) The gift of the Holy Spirit as an effect of baptism is presupposed by Paul (1 Co 12:13, 2 Co 1:22; also Eph 1:13, 4:30) . . . (d) In [connection] with the last two elements must be viewed the participation in Christ's death and resurrection, which is brought about through baptism (best stated in Ro 6:2ff)."

Conclusions

In no way is this evidence saying that those who believe the gospel but haven't fully obeyed the gospel have nothing. That would be a great error. This book does contend that because God cares for us, He desires to lead us continually deeper into the understanding and practice of His Word. Because of His great love, we can confidently allow Him to restore back into our lives and churches today what the enemy has stolen. Be encouraged to simply respond to the gospel in the same way early Christians embraced it, even if you have believed the gospel for a long time—and be faithful to teach the same thing to others, even if it means changing methods to be in agreement with the Scriptures. Responding (or re-responding) to the gospel with simple obedience is a win-win opportunity.

9

MISCONCEPTIONS

Because this book explores some biblical teachings that are different from many current church practices, it is reasonable to respectfully address some of them. Perhaps you have been thinking of one or more of these topics as you've studied these pages.

It can sometimes be difficult to accept more from God, especially when you have walked with Him for a long time. I have been there. My prayer is that this chapter will help clarify some potential disparities and make it easier to receive more of His good news. As long as we have faith to believe there is more of God's Word to learn and apply, we should look forward to Him sharing it with us.

Obeying the gospel: is it a works-based salvation?

It is understandable why some might look at obeying the gospel as somehow advocating salvation by works, rather than how we allow God to impart His saving righteousness by faith. This is especially important to address, considering how widespread the teaching of believing/trusting in the Lord without any need to apply the gospel has become. While believing in and trusting in the Lord is obviously essential to begin a relationship with Him, it is clear that early Christian converts always did so by identifying with each essential element of Christ's saving gospel, as we have seen. Had these early believers not trusted in the power of the gospel message, they would not have applied it to their lives.

Since Jesus washes our sins away by His blood as we obey His example and command of baptism—calling on His name to be saved—the work of imparting salvation comes from Him only, not us. Identifying with Jesus' burial cannot "earn" salvation; the saving is clearly God's work. We only allow God to impart His gift of salvation from sin by submitting to His instructions by faith.

The same is true when we are filled with the gift of God's Holy Spirit. This is also definitely His work. All we must do is receive it. This is why Acts 2:38 specifically calls the Holy Spirit a gift, for that is what His salvation is.

It is impossible for obeying the gospel to be a works-based salvation because salvation by works, in and of itself, is an impossibility. Each part of the gospel was designed by God to give us access to the gift of His saving grace. If this original, biblical pattern is salvation by works, then all converts in Scripture were saved by works, not by God's grace.

The thief on the cross

Many might look at the thief dying on the cross next to Christ as somehow exempting one from the need to apply the gospel for salvation. Jesus told this repentant man; "Truly I say to you, today you shall be with Me in Paradise." (See Luke 23:43)

There is a simple answer to this issue. The thief did not live (or die) during the period of Grace we live in now, but during the Law. Jesus was still in the process of completing His death, burial, and resurrection for humanity, so its accessibility was not yet available to the thief. However, Jesus was able to accurately judge the condemned man who confessed his sinfulness, and saw fit to extend paradise to him. Since there are no post-resurrection examples of anyone being saved without obeying the gospel, we can safely understand that it is God's will for New Testament believers to apply the good news message by faith, as we have carefully explored.

Baptism invoking the titles
"Father, Son, and Holy Spirit"

Many have said that as we baptize we are supposed to repeat the command given by Jesus in Matthew 28:19. I was raised with this tradition, and did not question it until I began to study the biblical record. Here are some practical points that helped me embrace the biblical-historical practice of being baptized in the name of Jesus Christ. I hope these conclusions will help as you consider your potential response to the information we have covered:

1. *To whom did Jesus give this command?* Who held the initial responsibility to obey the instructions of Matthew 28:19? Christ's apostles received this directive. The next question follows naturally.

2. *How did the apostles obey this command?* This was always done by using the name, and never by repeating the command. As we have seen, they understood the name was and always will be Jesus Christ. The next questions takes a bit more thought, but it helped me understand why the apostles didn't repeat the command, and their understanding of how to actually obey it.

3. *Is "Father," "Son" or "Holy Spirit" God's name?* The simple answer to each is no. While God is our Father, who sent His Son to die for us, and His Holy Spirit to indwell and lead us, these are not His saving name, but rather offices of authority and purpose He holds. All at one time, I can be a son, a father, a brother, and a husband. I am also a spirit-being (in addition to being flesh and blood). I can hold several different relationship-based positions or titles, but my name is Bradley A. Riley. If I am cashing a check and forget to sign "Bradley A. Riley" in the endorsement section on the back, the teller will return it and ask me to sign my name to make the transaction valid. I still wouldn't gain the intended benefit of the check if I wrote "My Name" instead of Bradley A. Riley. I know this is a simple analogy, but if we say to those we baptize, "I baptize you in the name of the Father, and of the Son, and of the Holy Ghost," have we used any name at all? I had to admit, the answer was no. This is why the apostles called on the name of Jesus Christ, which made the baptismal "transaction" of forgiveness of sins and "clothing" oneself with Christ valid.

4. *Is there any example in the Bible where even one convert was baptized by saying "Father, Son, and Holy Spirit?* This one really helped solidify my decision to be re-baptized in Jesus' name because, as we have seen and researched, no one in the Bible ever was baptized with this invocation.

5. *"It doesn't matter if I was baptized in the titles or in Jesus' name; either is correct."* What cleared up this question for me was to realize how this logic leads to a very slippery slope. If I could dismiss what I wanted from Scripture by saying "it doesn't matter," then where would it stop? The Bible does matter, a great deal. The name of Jesus does matter. After I realized I wasn't baptized scripturally during my previous ceremony, I was faced with the next question, which was to be a simple and very rewarding step of faith in Jesus Christ.

6. *Is being baptized or re-baptized in Jesus' name difficult to do?* When I asked myself this question, a new realization started to occur to me; w*hy would I not welcome this? If I did this, would there be a downside?* When I couldn't find a reason why I shouldn't be baptized in Jesus' name, I arranged to take this simple, but highly significant step. I have always cherished it. I know you will too, if you have not done so already.

7. *Can we call on any name other than Jesus Christ to save us from our sins?* The answer is obviously no. Since baptism is for the remission or forgiveness of sins, it makes sense to be re-baptized by calling on the name of the Lord.

Since Colossians 3:17 commands, "Whatever you do in word or deed, do all in the name of the Lord Jesus, giving thanks through Him to God the Father," and all post-resurrection believers were baptized in His name, my decision was clear. I wanted to do the same. If you aren't sure how you were baptized, or if you know it was not in the name of Jesus Christ, I hope you are motivated by your faith in God's Word to make the same rewarding decision.

The initial evidence of receiving the Holy Spirit

It would be remiss to overlook differing beliefs regarding receiving the Holy Spirit in the same way these converts did—with the initial evidence of speaking in tongues, and with tongues in general. I'm sure there might be more stances than will be addressed here, but below are some often-cited positions regarding this practice today, and how they might or might not fit the biblical model we have seen.

As we move into this subject, I cannot help but testify of things I have personally experienced and have seen hundreds and hundreds of times—people still consistently speak in tongues when they receive the Holy Spirit. With little research, you can see or read about it happening in church services or crusades around the globe. I have been in countless services and even in homes where young and old alike have experienced the same initial infilling—with the same biblical evidence. God is pouring out His Spirit across denominational boundaries as believers from all Christian persuasions as well as Muslims, Hindus, and many others are turning to Jesus Christ in thirsty faith—and being filled.

As we examine the positions below, I have attempted to allow Scripture to be the final authority for any conclusions arrived at. Here are three commonly held positions:

1. *Tongues have ceased, so tongues can no longer be the valid, initial evidence that one has received the Holy Spirit.* The verses of Scripture cited for this position are 1Corinthians 13:8-10, with a common explanation being that when the Bible was completed, there was no longer any need for tongues:

   Love never fails; but if there are gifts of prophecy, they will be done away; if there are tongues, they will cease; if there is knowledge, it will be done away. For we know in part and we prophesy in part; but when the perfect comes, the partial will be done away. (1Corinthians 13:8-10)

I'm not sure how this position explains the vast outpouring happening in the world today. Perhaps because it isn't happening within the specific groups that hold this belief, these feel that it isn't available for them presently. Regarding the interpretation that "tongues ceased" when the Bible was completed, notice carefully there will be several things "in part" that will cease (knowledge, tongues, prophecy) when that which is perfect (Greek: "complete") is come.

Has knowledge ceased? Have prophecies (many of which are yet to be fulfilled) ceased? You be the judge. When I was filled with the Holy Spirit, it was exactly the same experience as with those in the Bible. In Mark 16 Jesus Himself said that tongues were to be a sign that followed those that believe. He did not say that tongues were for apostles only, nor did He set an expiration date on tongues for the Church age.

Acts 2:39 says the promise of the Holy Ghost is for all who are "afar off." Jesus said in John 3 that the Spirit is like the wind and when people are born of the Spirit, you will hear the sound of it. Every time I see people receive the Holy Spirit, they speak with other languages, just as in the biblical accounts. The conclusion I came to when studying the 1Corinthians 13 passage above is that it refers to the return of Jesus Christ and the establishment of His government upon the Earth. This interpretation seems to be what "that which is perfect" references. Jesus Christ is the only perfect one the world has ever seen. When He returns, His government will supersede the gifts and realms of our current dispensation, which presently allow us to see through a glass darkly at best.

The fact that the promise of the Spirit is for all parallels Jesus' remarks in John 3 about there being a sound with all that are born of the Spirit. It would be inaccurate to deny the present-day outpouring of the Holy Spirit and the biblical witness of receiving it with the same evidence of tongues happening today.

> 2. *If there is an instance of speaking in tongues, there must always be an interpretation.* The Scriptures many look to for this position are in 1Corinthians as well:
>
>   All do not have gifts of healings, do they? All do not speak with tongues, do they? All do not interpret, do they? (1Corinthians 12:30)
>
>   If anyone speaks in a tongue, it should be by two or at the most three, and each in turn, and one must interpret; but if

there is no interpreter, he must keep silent in the church; and
let him speak to himself and to God. (1Corinthians 14:27-28)

The general theme of this part of Paul's letter to the Corinthian
church is that they needed order and oversight in practicing their
giftedness. Scripture declares in the same chapter that all things
should be done decently and in order. If someone speaks a
message in tongues to the church, it should absolutely be
interpreted. If there is no interpreter, the speaker should speak to
himself and God rather than bringing confusion by speaking to the
church. What many that hold the position above might not realize
is very easy to explain. There is a difference of administration
between the gift of tongues and speaking with tongues as the
initial evidence of receiving the gift of the Holy Spirit. In the same
way that not all have the gift of healing or interpretation of
tongues, neither do all have the gift of speaking a message in
tongues to the church.

Having observed and been involved with the operation of the
public gifts of tongues and interpretation of tongues for many
years, it is notably different from the tongues of someone
receiving the Holy Spirit or speaking to God in personal, Spirit-led
prayer. Notice when Paul directed the speaker to keep silence "in
the church," he also encouraged the persons involved to continue
speaking in tongues to themselves and God without interpretation.
It is clear that there was a distinct difference to Paul. His goal
seems to be stopping the confusion of public speaking without
interpretation, but not to stop personal Spirit-filled communication
with God.

The next position is a little difficult to understand scripturally, but
many hold it nevertheless:

3. *All tongues are of the devil.* While there isn't a biblical basis for
    this notion I can find, many hold this teaching and forbid
    tongues in their assemblies. Granted, I suppose there could be
    false tongues that could be inspired by demonic activity. The
    devil is a counterfeiter and impostor, so perhaps it makes
    sense that he would like to imitate or twist what God intends for
    our edification. One thing is for sure: it is impossible to have a
    counterfeit without a genuine. (For instance, the reason we've

never seen a fake US $25 bill is because there is no real one.) What I can find in the Bible to address the possibility that some tongues could be inspired of the devil is the following:

> Therefore I make known to you that no one speaking by the Spirit of God says, "Jesus is accursed"; and no one can say, "Jesus is Lord," except by the Holy Spirit. (1Corinthians 12:3)

If we speak by the Spirit of God, it is impossible to call Jesus accursed, and we cannot even say He is Lord but by the Spirit. If someone speaks in a language that is inspired by demonic power, he or she is obviously not speaking under the influence of God.

One word of caution I would share with anyone claiming that Holy Spirit-inspired tongues is of the devil, is to please keep in mind what Jesus said about speaking against the Holy Spirit:

> Therefore I say to you, any sin and blasphemy shall be forgiven people, but blasphemy against the Spirit shall not be forgiven. Whoever speaks a word against the Son of Man, it shall be forgiven him; but whoever speaks against the Holy Spirit, it shall not be forgiven him, either in this age or in the age to come. (Matthew 12:31-32)

In summary, perhaps it has not been stated better than by Paul:

> Therefore, my brethren, desire earnestly to prophesy, and do not forbid to speak in tongues. But all things must be done properly and in an orderly manner. (1Corinthians 14:39-40)

Benefits of speaking by the Spirit

While some believers don't see the need for this kind of praise or prayer, the Bible makes some very positive statements about speaking/praying in the Spirit. Some of the God-intended benefits of this kind of Spirit-infused prayer are referenced here:

Praying in the Holy Spirit builds faith

> But you, beloved, building yourselves up on your most holy faith, praying in the Holy Spirit, (Jude 20)

For one who speaks in a tongue does not speak to men but to God; for no one understands, but in his spirit he speaks mysteries. (1Corinthians 14:2)

For if I pray in a tongue, my spirit prays, but my mind is unfruitful. What is the outcome then? I will pray with the spirit and I will pray with the mind also; I will sing with the spirit and I will sing with the mind also. (1Corinthians 14:14-15)

The Spirit knows what to pray when we do not

In the same way the Spirit also helps our weakness; for we do not know how to pray as we should, but the Spirit Himself intercedes for us with groanings too deep for words; (Romans 8:26)

Scripture encourages us to pray in the Spirit as part of spiritual warfare

Therefore, take up the full armor of God, so that you will be able to resist in the evil day, and having done everything, to stand firm. With all prayer and petition pray at all times in the Spirit, and with this in view, be on the alert with all perseverance and petition for all the saints, (Ephesians 6:13, 18)

Ask and you shall receive

As simple as it might sound, many believers are receiving the Spirit today by merely beginning to ask for it. As mentioned previously, these individuals often never saw the need to ask God to be Spirit-filled—because of being taught they automatically had the Spirit at the point of belief. Growing up, I had never really considered that I should ask to be filled with the Holy Spirit, but this is what Jesus told us to do in Luke 9, and to expect in John 7. As the Bible teaches, I had not because I asked not. When I asked, I received.

I realize that some of the positions we have visited may be deeply held by many sincere believers. It can be especially difficult to consider there is more to being Spirit-filled after already believing in Jesus for a long time. If this is your case, allow yourself to consider these possibilities:

- Is it possible I am reading this now because God desires to share more of Himself with me than ever before?
- Perhaps God has seen my sincere love for Him and wants to respond by pouring His Spirit into me with a greater depth and intimacy than I have yet to experience.
- Would God want to give me more of His Spirit, or less?

Welcoming the simplicity of the gospel

Obeying the gospel of Jesus Christ is the plain and established scriptural method for believers to invite God's redeeming grace into their lives. We have seen believers in the Bible consistently apply His death through repentance, His burial by being baptized in His name, and His resurrection by receiving His Holy Spirit. Today, we have an easy opportunity to follow their clear examples by faith.

For many, this biblical plan might seem antiquated, especially if it is not familiar. However, we must not forget that God is in the process of restoring all things until Christ's return—and allowing Him to restore this part of His Word for us is a good thing. Would our loving Father want anything less than to re-establish more of His Word for His children?

Jesus' gospel plan is a simple one; it only requires faith to act upon it. Please be encouraged to embrace this scriptural pattern for yourself, and confidently share it with those inside your circle of influence.

10

FOOD FOR THOUGHT – CLOSING REMARKS

As we conclude in our final chapter, I would like to thank you for making the journey through these pages. I hope you have received something wonderful, and trust you will demonstrate faith by acting upon these Scriptures if you have not done so already. As mentioned in the introduction, *What Happened to Obeying the Gospel* is not intended to be offensive, and I sincerely hope it has not come across as such to you. The objective is merely to "contend earnestly for the faith which was once for all handed down to the saints" as we are charged to do by Jude's epistle.

In an age where standing for truth is becoming increasingly rare and inconvenient, be encouraged to stand for obeying the gospel according to the Bible, even if it means standing alone for a season. Cultural influence may change people and even churches, but even the strongest culture will never change God's Word. Whatever your culture is, don't be afraid to take this gospel-applying message and dive right into it.

In closing, I would like to offer a few more items to encourage your thoughts and actions. Wherever God takes you, enjoy the journey of discovery as you walk with His hand in yours, enthusiastically embracing where He leads.

A required number of witnesses

> A single witness shall not rise up against a man on account of any iniquity or any sin which he has committed; on the evidence of two or three witnesses a matter shall be confirmed. (Deuteronomy 19:15)

Why does the Bible provide so many "witnesses" of obeying the gospel? God is firmly establishing a practice—to show any other witness to be either true or unfaithful.

A personal relationship

It is true that anyone can have a relationship with God. However, just because we have a relationship with God doesn't necessarily mean we are in right standing with Him. Even Satan has a relationship with God (i.e., access, communication, influence—see Job 1-2, but no right standing—see Revelation 12:10). We have right standing with God through applying His saving gospel as revealed by the Bible.

Who else is father, son, and spirit?

As unusual as it might sound, did you know that the devil is a father, a son and a spirit—but those titles are not his name? They simply describe him. He is the father of lies according to John 8:44, the son of the morning in Isaiah 14:12 and referred to as an unclean spirit in places like Luke 11:24. Is using a name really so important? If the name is Jesus Christ, then yes, it is:

> And there is salvation in no one else; for there is no other name under heaven that has been given among men by which we must be saved. (Acts 4:12)

Trusting Jesus as our personal Savior

If we have taken the step of trusting Jesus to be our personal Savior, we can also safely trust His Word that teaches we should repent of our sins and call on His saving name for salvation from sins at our baptism. If we won't take these simple steps of faith, we should probably ask ourselves, "Are we really trusting?" These are small and easy steps of trust to take—and ones with powerful and lasting significance.

Demonstrating faith accesses effectiveness

Believing is the irreplaceable foundation of our relationship with God. If we didn't believe, we would never have reason to demonstrate faith. We can know our faith is real when it prompts us to do something about it. If believing alone were sufficient to apply the gospel, New Testament believers would have stopped there. It was *because* they believed that they consistently obeyed this saving message by applying each part of it by faith. We can enjoy the intended benefits of the gospel with the same response today. Here are some simple examples that mirror this line of reasoning:

- If we believe penicillin eliminates infection—we must take it to be cured
- If we are convinced food stops hunger—we must eat it to be nourished
- If drinking water solves thirst—we must do so to be quenched
- If an umbrella will keep us dry in the rain—we must open it to remain dry

God's Word and personal experience convinced me that if I believed the gospel is God's power of salvation—I must demonstrate my faith by applying each part of it to receive its intended effectiveness.

Saved by . . .

God has mercifully given us many things for our salvation, and all of them are gifts of His grace. To say we don't need them all would be a mistake. While it might be popular to look to a favorite verse about salvation, we would be negligent to exclude what the others declare. Here are some of the things that save us according to the Bible, along with their references:

Faith - Luke 7:50 Ephesians 2:8

Grace - Acts 15:11, Ephesians 2:8, 2Timothy 1:9, Titus 2:11

Endurance - Matthew 10:22

Jesus - John 3:17, 10:19, 1Thessalonians 5:9

Belief in Jesus - John 3:16, Acts 16:31, Romans 10:9

Belief in the Word - Luke 8:12

Jesus' words - John 5:34

Calling on the name of the Lord - Acts 2:21, Romans 10:13

Obeying Jesus - Hebrews 5:9

The name of Jesus - Acts 4:12

Jesus' blood - Romans 5:9

Jesus' life - Romans 5:10

The words of the apostles - Acts 11:14, 1Thessalonians 2:16, 1Corinthians 1:21, Acts 16:17

The gospel - 1Corinthians 15:1-2, Romans 1:16, Ephesians 1:13

Obeying the gospel - Acts 2:38-40

Baptism - Mark 16:16, 1Peter 3:21

Hope - Romans 8:24

Love of the truth - 2Thessalonians 2:10

Washing of regeneration and the renewing of the Holy Spirit - Titus 3:5

Sanctification by the Spirit and faith in the truth - 2Thessalonians 2:13

Difficulty - 1Peter 4:18

Drawing near to God - Hebrews 7:25

The implanted word - James 2:21

Teaching - 1Timothy 4:16

The wisdom of the Word of God - 2Timothy 3:15

Implementing obedience to the gospel

You might be a believer that would sincerely like to see your church accept and practice what you have seen in this book. If so, I would encourage you to fast, pray and respectfully approach your church leadership with this information. Ask God to help them have hearts to prayerfully and sincerely consider what you have seen from the Bible. Continue to pray for them (as I hope you are regularly doing) while they consider the opportunity of carefully leading your congregation into what might be unfamiliar biblical territory.

If you are a pastor, you might be thinking, "I would like to implement this within our church, but how will I go about it?" I don't have all the answers, but here are some safe bets: it will take patience, courage, conviction, and it might cost something—initially. When people love the Word though, they will accept it and respect you for loving them enough to stand up for its truths. Let your key leaders and influencers absorb this information. Fast, pray, and have them do the same. Allow God to do for them what you've allowed Him to do in your heart. Remember that God has you in a position to lead for a reason. As you pray about your course of action, think of these courageous examples:

Josiah received God's Word he was previously unaware of and led Judah bravely into what it commanded, despite any upheaval it may have caused. The Bible remembers his legacy in glowing terms. His example is a blueprint to look to today.

Peter acted fearlessly, despite Jewish tradition, when he heard from God in Acts 10, and the Gentiles entered the kingdom of God.

Saul heard from God on the Damascus road, and bravely changed his beliefs to agree with what God showed him. Things were rocky for a while, but because of his willingness to obey God rather than man, we received much of the New Testament writings we have today. I'm sure he would say he made the right decision.

Abraham left an established (and likely comfortable) lifestyle in Ur to follow God, becoming the father of God's chosen people on the Earth. His choice changed the course of history for all those who would walk by faith in the future.

Moses went against his royal upbringing and left the palaces of Egypt to follow God. Because of his courage, the Hebrew nation was liberated from the bondage of slavery, received the Word of God, and eventually inherited their Promised Land.

Apollos was eloquent, mighty in the Scriptures and instructed in the way of the Lord. When Aquila and Priscilla showed him the way of the Lord more perfectly in Acts 18, he received it and preached this message alongside the apostles.

Luther was viewed as a radical when he nailed his 95 Theses to the doors of Castle Church in 1517. Today he is admired as one God used to restore the important scriptural truth: "The just shall live by faith."

To those who look to the Pope for leadership

The apostle Peter, regarded by many as the first Pope of the Catholic Church, did not apply the gospel as current Catholic doctrine suggests (sprinkling in the titles Father, Son, Holy Spirit). Instead, he baptized by immersion in the name of Jesus Christ. As we saw in our reference section, other popes also approved baptism in Jesus' name. Because of these original biblical and historical examples, precious Catholic believers also have precedent to be re-baptized, just as the Ephesian disciples were in Acts 19, calling on the name of the Lord Jesus Christ.

We must build according to the pattern

If God was specific with His instructions to Moses about building the Tabernacle "according to the pattern," He does not abandon the necessity of this type of faithfulness with the New Testament plan. This is especially true when we understand the Tabernacle was a shadow of heavenly things:

> Who serve a copy and shadow of the heavenly things, just as Moses was warned by God when he was about to erect the tabernacle; for, "SEE," He says, "THAT YOU MAKE all things ACCORDING TO THE PATTERN WHICH WAS SHOWN YOU ON THE MOUNTAIN." (Hebrews 8:5)

Calling on His name

If we are sick or in danger, whose name do we instinctively call on? When we are desperate for help from God, what name do we speak in prayer? Hopefully, it is the name above every name— Jesus Christ. Why then shouldn't we call on this name at the most important faith-response to the gospel; our baptism? This is particularly reliable since it was the only invocation given at every post-resurrection baptism in the Bible.

In light of all Jesus has done for us, it is so simple to be baptized or re-baptized in the wonderful, saving name of Jesus Christ to fully obey the gospel. This standard Bible practice is more than reasonable once we become aware of it. When we love the name of Jesus more than any other, it makes it even easier.

Jesus Christ, the same yesterday, today, and forever

Consider again that if Jesus Christ, the very God of the universe manifested in flesh, had to die, be buried, and rise again before *He* could ascend to Heaven, how much more should we take the opportunity to identify with each saving element of His example to receive their full effectiveness? This is why obeying the gospel is so important, and why God wants to restore this simple pattern back to us today. We only need to look at the conversion accounts in Scripture to have all the evidence we need of this profound New Testament truth.

A final word

One of the most important signs of our healthy relationship with God is that He continues to lead us into more of His Word. Having faith to apply it is the simple evidence of our trust in Him. When we see there is more we can receive, it deserves our enthusiastic faith. If it is in His Word, it was there all along, even though it might seem new or unfamiliar at first. If you recognize the meaning of obeying the gospel as never before, it is very likely that God has seen your heartfelt love for Him, and has simply responded by bringing you the opportunity to receive more of His wonderful Word.

Throughout history, God has worked through countless people to help restore truths that were there all along, and I believe He would love to use your life to do the same for others. Please don't allow the enemy the satisfaction of preventing this restoration for you or those who are under your care. Why wait? There is no reason to deprive ourselves of the lasting benefits of simple obedience. You'll be so glad you did. God bless!

ABOUT THE AUTHOR

If you are hoping to read something impressive about the author here, you might be in for a disappointment. The plain truth is that Bradley Riley comes from a background of very deep sin, and owes anything and everything good in his life to our amazing Savior.

Since we cannot give something that we have not first received, it would be a mistake to take credit for discovering a truth as profound as obeying the gospel—which was there long ago. If God can use someone like the author to help bring more of His good news to the people He loves, that is a great honor and privilege. Let's just give the credit to whom it belongs, the Lord Jesus Christ.

Therefore, there is no great spiritual pedigree offered here to provoke your admiration, just many years of grateful service to the Body of Christ. If there is anything worth boasting about, it has to be God's amazing grace that saves us from our sins and equips us to share the good news Christ came to give us all.